Remaining Chickasaw in Indian Territory

Remaining Chickasaw in Indian Territory, 1830s–1907

WENDY ST. JEAN

THE UNIVERSITY OF ALABAMA PRESS

Tuscaloosa

Typeface: Granjon

∞

The paper on which this book is printed meets the minimum requirements of
American National Standard for Information Sciences—Permanence of Paper
for Printed Library Materials, ANSI Z39.48-1984.

Library of Congress Cataloging-in-Publication Data

St. Jean, Wendy.
Remaining Chickasaw in Indian Territory, 1830s–1907 / Wendy St. Jean.
p. cm.
Includes bibliographical references and index.
ISBN 978-0-8173-1725-6 (cloth : alk. paper) — ISBN 978-0-8173-5642-2
(paper : alk. paper) — ISBN 978-0-8173-8519-4 (electronic) 1. Chickasaw
Indians—Oklahoma—History—19th century. 2. Chickasaw Indians—
Oklahoma—Politics and government—19th century. 3. Chickasaw Indians—
Oklahoma—Ethnic identity—History—19th century. 4. Choctaw Nation of
Oklahoma—History—19th century. 5. Chickasaw Indians—Government
relations—History—19th century. 6. Sovereignty—History—19th century.
7. Indian Territory—History. 8. Oklahoma—Ethnic relations—History—
19th century. 9. Social conflict—Oklahoma—History—19th century. 10.
Oklahoma—Social conditions—19th century. I. Title.
E99.C55S7 2011
976.004′97386—dc22

2010031634

Cover art courtesy of Shawn He Yuxun.

To my parents, Janine and John St. Jean

Contents

Acknowledgments

I owe debts to many people. My parents, my husband, and my daughters for their moral support. My mentors, Chickasaw historian Richard Green, Karen Kupperman, David LaVere, Nancy Shoemaker, and Joseph Hall, for their encouragement and review of my various writings over the years. A special thanks to William Welge, Phyllis Adams, Sharron Standifer Ashton, Michael Lovegrove, and the rest of the staff and researchers at the Indian Archives of the Oklahoma Historical Society, who have been there since the beginning of my research. Other very helpful persons include librarian Joseph Frawley of the Mashantucket Pequot Research library and Sarah Barnard of the American Antiquarian Society. Chapters of this book were reviewed at different stages by Professor Laurel Davis-Delano of Springfield College in Massachusetts, and by Professor Saul Lerner and Professor Miriam Joyce of Purdue University Calumet. I would also like to thank Richard Rupp, the chair of the history and political science department of Purdue University Calumet, for granting me course releases to complete this book and other publications.

Remaining Chickasaw in Indian Territory, 1830s–1907

Introduction

Challenges to Chickasaw Sovereignty

Historically, the Chickasaws lived within the watershed of the Tombigbee River, a territory that today includes mostly western Tennessee and northern Mississippi. Before the Chickasaws' emigration to Indian Territory, their definition of themselves was shaped by ancestry, clan affiliation, and their reputation as fierce defenders of their homeland. Even today the Chickasaw national government's Web site boasts that the Chickasaws are an unconquered people. They were united in the eighteenth century by the French threat to their survival and by their small numbers and relative homogeneity. Outnumbered by enemies and eager to build their population base, the Chickasaw Nation was an inclusive one. Many Chickasaw families adopted captives and refugees from the Natchez, Chakiuma, Yazoo, and other Indian tribes. European traders who married Chickasaw women were given limited privileges, and their children were recognized as full citizens of the tribe.

Although combined armies of the French, the Choctaws, and Canadian Indians proved unable to defeat them, the Chickasaws, like their Indian neighbors with larger populations, capitulated to U.S. and state pressures in the early nineteenth century to cede their lands and begin anew in Indian Territory.[1] The Chickasaws' prime, fertile land was eagerly sought after by white cotton planters. Combined pressure from Mississippi, the federal government, and legions of white squatters drove the leaders of the Chickasaws to sign the Franklin Removal Treaty (1830) with the United States. They thereby ceded their homeland and agreed to move to land set aside for them and the other four of the Five Tribes (Cherokees, Creeks, Choctaws, and Seminoles) in present-day Oklahoma. Soon afterward whites overrode the Chickasaws' ancestral lands, but the tribe still lacked land in Indian Territory to call its own. By the time the Chickasaws agreed to relocate, all the portions of land set aside for Indians were already taken. The Chickasaws purchased lands from the Choctaw Nation, but the area was isolated from commerce and inhabited by hostile western tribes. As a condition for granting the Chickasaws a new home, the Choctaws demanded unification, stripping the Chickasaws of their distinct citizenship. Despite the Chickasaws' cultural similarities to the Choctaws—from shared healing ceremonies and burial traditions to *pashofa* (hominy with meat) feasts and ball games—the Chickasaws stressed their distinctive identity and their dissatisfaction with their minority representation in the Choctaw government.

Before the Chickasaws could shape their district of the Choctaw Nation to reflect their national goals and aspirations, they had to make their lands safe for Chickasaw families. The first Chickasaw immigrants faced assaults by Comanche and Osage bands that regarded them as intruders. The Chickasaws also faced Texans' suspicion that they were criminally involved in the western Indians' raids. Although some Chickasaw merchants benefited from the Comanche trade in captives and stolen horses, the Chickasaw Nation eventually joined Texans in making war against the western Indians. The Chickasaws took a hard stand against the western Indians in part to defend their families, slaves, and livestock; however, no lesser motive was to forestall Texan Rangers from including them in their indiscriminate war against Indians on the borders of Texas.

In Indian Territory the Chickasaws struggled for a new definition of themselves that was rooted in their distinctive heritage, represented by their hereditary chiefs. Chickasaw efforts to restore their old government based on ancestry failed because the tribe's U.S. agent insisted that the Chickasaw Nation adopt a republican, electoral system. As a trade-off, the Chickasaw government received federal recognition of its sovereignty and was freed from minority status in the Choctaw government in 1855. The Chickasaw constitution of 1856 called for an elected governor in place of a hereditary chief to head the nation.

After the American Civil War, the federal government demanded land cessions from the defeated Chickasaw Confederates for railroads and reservations for western Indians. The Treaty of 1866 ending Chickasaw participation in the war included an ominous clause: it stated that once the Chickasaws vanished, their lands would revert to the federal government, with tracts reserved for railroad companies to transport a multitude of white settlers into their nation. The Treaty of 1866 also stipulated that the Chickasaws adopt their former slaves as Chickasaw citizens or pay for their ejection from their lands.

Over time, Chickasaw leaders came to view U.S. officials' demand for the adoption of freedpeople as another veiled attempt to destroy their tribal sovereignty by admitting a large group of outsiders to full citizenship. Since many freedpeople spoke Chickasaw and were raised in Chickasaw culture, their existence among the Chickasaws was not problematic until the freedpeople pushed for a redefinition of their status as full Indian citizens. Most Chickasaws tolerated them as neighbors and landholders, but were unwilling to see them enfranchised because of their association with railroads and other interest groups that wanted to abolish the Chickasaws' communal land base. The freedpeople, influenced by enterprising citizenship lawyers, came to believe that they were entitled to more and more of the Chickasaws' resources and inheritance. The Chickasaws demanded the exclusive right to govern the lands in Indian Territory that they had purchased with the proceeds from their Mississippi homeland.

By the 1870s thousands of outsiders made claims to Chickasaw property and natural resources. In the Chickasaw Nation, as in the other nations of the Five Tribes, one finds a variety of persons who "should not" have been there. Whites, blacks, and Comanches, among other western tribes, entered the nation in a variety of guises: as traders, intruders, outlaws, tenants, cowhands, and spouses.[2] After the Civil War, these groups flooded the Chickasaw Nation. Soon the population of noncitizens surpassed that of the Chickasaw people, and the small, beleaguered nation reacted defensively. Chickasaw legislators passed measures to regulate these groups and, if possible, remove them from their territory. Coming in ever-larger numbers, whites refused to submit to Chickasaw laws. To curtail white immigration, the Chickasaw government levied a substantial tax on noncitizens and demanded U.S. military assistance in ejecting those whites who refused to register and pay the permit fee. The U.S. government recognized the Chickasaws' right to tax intruders, but Washington officials provided very little assistance in confronting this mounting problem.

Intermarried whites became a problem because they were the least communally oriented tribal members. They, their family members, and business partners engrossed large acres of tribal land and invited other whites to rent range and farmland from them. They generally favored railroads, allotment (the subdivision and privatization of tribal lands), and other measures that would increase their personal wealth. The fortunes of subsistence-oriented Chickasaw farmers were of no concern to them. The Chickasaw government restrained the political influence of intermarried whites by temporarily disfranchising them.

Chickasaw leaders counted on their national education system, their final bastion of sovereignty, as the means to preserve their history and instill national pride in their youth. Through Chickasaw-run schools, they retained the Chickasaw language, fostered Chickasaw patriotism, and provided employment to encourage the best and brightest students to remain in the tribe. On one hand, their curriculum emulated the leading American schools of the day; however, the schools also perpetuated a nationality grounded in tribal history and the students' common experiences, some of them triumphant, others reflective of abuse at the hands of whites. Group solidarity and ethnic cohesion, features of the education system since the 1820s, would be assaulted by the federal government's mandates to assimilate other Indians, whites, and black students into Chickasaw schools.

In the 1890s the Dawes Commission (named after its chair, Senator Henry L. Dawes) replaced Chickasaw sovereignty with congressional authority by imposing its definition of who was a Chickasaw citizen. The Chickasaws argued that they alone knew who belonged to them and who did not. They rightly feared that the Dawes Commission would include in its grants of citizenship many fraudulent claims by opportunistic whites. After the Dawes Commission completed its rolls, the U.S. government subdivided the Chickasaws' lands, disbanded the Chickasaws' schools, and terminated the Chickasaws' legislature to ready the tribe for incorporation into the state of Oklahoma.

As these episodes suggest, the Chickasaw government adopted a fairly consistent strategy of dealing with outsiders by creating more and more barriers to tribal citizenship and its benefits. This is a study of the Chickasaw Nation's struggle, in the wake of encroachments by the federal government and groups of noncitizen immigrants, to restrict tribal membership and assert its flagging sovereignty in the nineteenth century.

In defense of a separate Indian nationhood, Chickasaw politicians of the National Party, which predominated following the Civil War, took an oppositional stance not just against U.S. citizens but against other Indians and African Americans. Under the National Party's leadership, the Chickasaw government increasingly rejected non-Indian groups' claims to membership in its nation and reduced newcomers' access to the privileges enjoyed by Chickasaw citizens. At the turn of the century, as its nationhood drew to a close, the Chickasaw Nation turned to blood ancestry as the only marker that could preserve tribal members' resources in their own hands.

A persistent and legitimate threat that stalked the Chickasaw Nation in the last decades of the nineteenth century was that the U.S. government would strip away the tribe's lands under the pretext that there was no longer a recognizable body of Indians living there. U.S. congressmen, swayed by corporate representatives and whites eager to open Indian Territory to white settlement, portrayed the Chickasaw people as barely distinguishable from whites. Lewis N. Hornbeck, the editor of a boomer newspaper in the Chickasaw Nation, told this anecdote to Congress: when a man in Indian Territory asked him how he liked the territory, he replied, "It would very much assist one to have the Indians labeled, so that one would not make a mistake. Why . . . I have met men since I came here who said they were Indian who did not look any more like an Indian than you do. Imagine my surprise when he told me that he was an Indian, being an eighth blood, and a member of the Chickasaw legislature."[3]

If Indians were not recognizable (to outsiders), then how could they be Indians? This was a question no one had asked until whites sought to displace the tribes from their lands in Indian Territory.

In the late nineteenth century, most Americans assumed that "at best the Indian nation was a transitional state for Native people on the way to assimilation."[4] While U.S. officials encouraged Indians to shed outward signs of their culture, they also used the Five Tribes' successful emulation of white society as an excuse to rob them of their independent status and lands. As editor Hornbeck testified: "Generally, when we speak of Indians, we mean savages, or blanket Indians, who live in tepees and subsist by the chase. In that sense, there are no Indians at all in the Indian Territory."[5] Congressional hearings abounded with white claims to Chickasaw lands on the basis of there not being any more "real Indians."[6] While such an image of the Chickasaws was (and continues to be) inaccurate, it was emphasized in order to despoil the Indians of their land and heritage. Many whites presented statistics designed to demonstrate the Indians' "vanishing" state. For example, in 1893 a reporter for the *Purcell Register* underlined the fact that the Chickasaws constituted a minority in their own land: "This fair land is held by a nation of about 6,800 citizens. These dwell amidst a population of over 40,000 non-citizens."[7]

Overall, the story of the Chickasaw Nation in the nineteenth century is one of a dramatic struggle reflecting the Chickasaw government's determination to preserve tribal heritage by constantly redefining Chickasaw identity. On the other hand, political rivalries revealed some Chickasaws' desire to enrich themselves at the cost of tribal survival. There were always members of the Chickasaw Nation willing to sacrifice elements of their traditional culture for individual political power and wealth.

Despite the nation's small population and internal divisions, the Chickasaw government managed to hold on to a measure of independence and inheritance longer and more effectively than its Indian neighbors. In state and federal courts and in the court of public opinion, the Chickasaws challenged noncitizens' claims and sometimes won privileges that other Indian nations surrendered without a fight. For example, the Chickasaw Nation delayed Indian Removal the longest, got the best payment for its southeastern lands, secured the right to tax and use force against white intruders, excluded intermarried whites from voting in critical national elections (1880s through the 1890s), surrendered its schools last, and was the only tribe to gain compensation for allotments that the U.S. government granted to freedpeople. The Chickasaws' leadership methods and attempts to redefine tribal membership helped them to accomplish these political and legal feats.

In general, the multifaceted attacks on the Chickasaws' sovereignty strengthened their sense of national pride and their resolve to fight. The Chickasaw government resolutely opposed U.S. policies that attempted to merge the Chickasaws indiscriminately with other Indians, blacks, and whites. Admittedly, the Chickasaws' Progressive Party members identified with the dominant industrializing society, and they undermined their nation by advocating a change in the tribe's status. The Chickasaw Nation's last hope was that the U.S. Supreme Court would back its treaty rights despite pressure from intruders, corporate agents, and a mostly hostile Congress. But it was too late for the Supreme Court to reverse the tide of white settlers and decades of expansionist U.S. policy. U.S. justices validated some of the Chickasaws' monetary claims but not their right to continue as an independent nation.

I

Struggle for Independence from the Choctaw Nation, 1837–1855

A reporter for the *Arkansas Gazette* explained the rationale of U.S. policy makers who wanted to relocate the Chickasaws and the Choctaws in the same section of Indian Territory: "The two nations, from contiguity and intermarriage, have become so closely identified in language, in habits, in manners, and in customs, that they could not well live apart from each other."[1] The federal government failed to understand the national rivalry between the two tribes, and the U.S. policy of compelling them to live together under a single government resulted in much bitterness. By 1856 the Chickasaw government had drawn up its own constitution, which marked the nations' separate lands and defined their tribal membership.

The Chickasaws and Choctaws were very similar in cultural attributes. Their mutually intelligible languages derived from Muskogean, and they shared a common migration story, in which they followed a sacred leaning pole from the far West to their homes in the Southeast. Their societies were organized matrilineally (meaning that ancestry was traced only through the mother's line), political power was decentralized and village based, and they worshipped the sun for its ability to create and sustain life.

However, the Chickasaws and Choctaws were longtime military rivals, dating back at least to the late seventeenth century. As a consequence of their trade alliance with the British, the Chickasaws warred on the Choctaws to secure captives for the South Carolina slave trade (1690s–1715), and after the French armed the Choctaws, the Chickasaws faced continual assaults by the far more numerous Choctaws, partly in vengeance and party as a result of French bounties for Chickasaw scalps.

After peace between France and Great Britain came in 1763, the Chickasaws and Choctaws put aside their old enmities based on revenge and began intermarrying more widely. The Chickasaws may have encouraged these marital unions to strengthen their tribe. At that time, the Chickasaw Nation numbered only eight hundred warriors and about two thousand people altogether. In the 1790s, in diplomatic negotiations with the Spanish in Louisiana, the Chickasaws emphasized that if they went to war against another people, they could count on military assistance from the Choctaws. Because Francisco Luis Carondelet, governor of Spanish Louisiana from 1791 to 1797, observed that the Chickasaw Nation would "always draw along the Choctaws with it" in war, he intervened to end the Creek-Chickasaw War of 1795 before the Creeks inadvertently killed any Choctaws married to Chickasaw women.[2]

At the same time that security needs and family bonds drew the tribes together, the Chickasaw and Choctaw governments' negotiations with the United States generated distinctive tribal interests. The Treaty of Hopewell (1786) signaled the beginning of the Five Tribes' relationship with the new American Republic. Since that time, the Chickasaws and Choctaws had negotiated separate land sales with Congress. Now being a Chickasaw or a Choctaw meant more than an ethnic classification; it conferred tribal-based entitlement to monetary settlements. The U.S. government differentiated the Chickasaw and Choctaw governments' financial and political interests again in the 1830s with separate Indian Removal treaties. The Chickasaws secured better terms for the sale of their homelands than the Choctaws and put more away for the education of their children.

Both the Chickasaws and the Choctaws jealously guarded their homelands, wary of further land sales. In his first annual address to Congress (1829), President Andrew Jackson announced that he was going to get tough on the southern Indians who refused to move west. Encouraged by Jackson, in 1830 the state of Mississippi extended its criminal laws over the Chickasaws and the Choctaws and outlawed tribal governments. The tribes were to expect no protection from the federal government, which wanted to break down their resistance to moving west. Jackson's treaty commissioners warned that the whites could summon thousands of soldiers to compel the Indians to submit to Mississippi's laws.

Congress followed suit with the Indian Removal Act (1830), which gave whites in the surrounding states a free hand to drive the Indians out of their homelands. Under the terms of the act, the federal government negotiated separate treaties with each of the Five Tribes detailing the conditions for the sale of their eastern lands and the purchase of new lands in Indian Territory.

The Chickasaws' departure from northern Mississippi was delayed several years by their failure to find satisfactory western lands. The Chickasaws' Franklin Treaty (1830) provided for the cession of all remaining Chickasaw lands in exchange for a tract west of the Mississippi River. However, it stipulated that if "a country suitable to their wants and conditions cannot be found, then . . . this treaty and all its provisions shall be considered null and void."[3] The Chickasaw leaders believed that they had outsmarted U.S. agents by inserting this provision in their treaty.

Levi Colbert was the key leader in negotiations with the U.S. government. The son of James Logan Colbert, a Georgia trader married into the Chickasaw Nation in 1758, and Noe, a Chickasaw woman, Colbert was about a generation older than his counterparts among neighboring tribes. He lacked a formal Christian education, having been raised by his mother in the Chickasaw way. His father's main influence may have been teaching him how white men think and do business, as well as broken English and a smattering of French. Like the planter elites of other tribes, the members of the Colbert family owned hundreds of horses, livestock, slaves, and a wide array of farming implements, which they attained through inheritance, trade, military service, and as gifts from U.S. agents. The Colberts defended the Chickasaws' traditional social structure, which recognized them as full members of the tribe based on matrilineal descent and propelled them to power as advisors to the principal clan chief, or *minko*.

Unlike his brothers William and George, who earned titles and fame for their military service to the tribe and the U.S. Army, Levi Colbert preferred to distinguish himself in the political sector. Colbert's Indian name, Itawamba, is translated as "bench chief," a reference to the fact that he was accorded the honor of sitting on a bench rather than the ground. He signed with his X mark the Treaty of 1805, an outright land cession to the United States, and his first appearance on the public scene. In 1812 Colbert came to power through a traditional channel, as counselor to Minko Chehopistee. When the younger, less politically experienced Minko Ishtehotopa succeeded Chehopistee in 1820, Colbert gained more prominence in the tribe's political life.

Colbert signed successive land cession treaties in 1816, 1818, and 1830 (the Franklin Treaty). The Treaty of 1816 paid Colbert $4,500 for redistribution to those Chickasaws displaced by the land sales. Levi and his brother George also secured land reserves for themselves and their heirs on the Tennessee and Tombigbee rivers. The Treaty of 1818 paid off a sizeable debt of William Colbert, amounting to $1,115, and reserved a salt lick to Levi Colbert, as trustee for his nation; it also provided for monetary awards to the Colbert brothers. Colbert expected full compensation from the U.S. government for his real estate investments. His home in Cotton Gin Port (in present-day Monroe, Mississippi) was filled with the comforts of life, as was the inn he ran for travelers near Buzzard Roost Spring on the Natchez Trace parkway. The granting of cash payments, reserves, and other favors to chiefs typified Indian treaties at this time and served as a way for U.S. commissioners to simultaneously weaken the chiefs' resistance and compromise their reputations among their people. However, no outright cash payments were made in the Franklin Treaty of 1830, or later treaties, due to the vigilance of the Chickasaw people, who passed legislation to outlaw monetary compensation, which had come to be viewed as bribery.

In 1827 Indian commissioner Thomas McKenney met privately with Colbert and his main supporters to discuss the tribe's relocation to Indian Territory. McKenney was a personal friend and had charge of Winchester's (1810–80), one of Colbert's sons, education. McKenney acknowledged Colbert in a powerful and visible role (one the U.S. government helped to create for its own purposes) as the official "Speaker of the Nation." Before, Colbert had been the minko's spokesman, and not even the minko presumed to speak for "the nation." Colbert made no commitment to western relocation at this meeting, but he agreed to send a party to view the lands in the West. The Chickasaws chose Colbert to lead an exploring party in 1828 to view a potential new site for settlement in Indian Territory. The members of the expedition found no lands there that equaled their fertile ones in the Mississippi River Valley.

Colbert expressed interest in Caddo lands, Osage lands, and a tract in what is now the Panhandle of Texas, but Chickasaw agent Benjamin Reynolds dismissed these choices as unobtainable.[4] The U.S. government expected to consolidate all the Indians into Indian Territory with the goal of confining Indians in the West to as small a space as possible. The fertile agricultural lands identified by Chickasaw exploring parties would be reserved for whites. So the Chickasaw Nation's delayed departure from Mississippi meant only that it would not get its choice of the marginal farmlands that the government offered the Indians for resettlement in present-day Oklahoma.

The aging Levi Colbert grew ill and was unable to attend further treaty negotiations. He protested the Treaty of Pontotoc, negotiated during his absence in 1832, on the grounds that it would profit the acculturated minority to the disadvantage of the less educated majority. An amended treaty, the Washington Articles of Confederation (1834), created a new governing body for the Chickasaws, the Commission of Seven, headed by Minko Ishtehotopa. The commission (the other members were Levi Colbert, George Colbert, Martin Colbert [Levi's son], Isaac Alberson, Henry Love, and Benjamin Love) oversaw the survey of Chickasaw land and designated who would receive land and how much. In 1834 the actual assignment of individual lots began.[5] That year Levi Colbert died on his way to Washington, D.C., to lobby for more provisions to protect illiterate Chickasaws from graft and other unfair dealings. He did not live to see the Chickasaws' forced relocation to Indian Territory.

Before the Chickasaws found a western home, the U.S. government's policy of Indian Removal began with the division of tribal lands into individual allotments. U.S. agents sold the surplus land and applied the proceeds to a fund for the tribe, part of which would be used to resettle the tribe in Indian Territory. Chickasaw protests over the corrupt reservation system that resulted from the treaty led the United States to resume negotiations with the Chickasaws and the Choctaws and to press for the Chickasaws' integration into the Choctaw Nation.

Several Chickasaws with Choctaw spouses removed with Choctaw immigration parties to Indian Territory in the winter of 1831. General John Coffee applauded this circumstance and urged the secretary of war to "carry with them" as many intermarried Chickasaws as they could, hoping that they would use their influence to bring about "an agreement for the Chickasaw to settle on the Choctaw lands upon some terms or other."[6] The Choctaw government was unreceptive to the idea, however. Leaders bluntly informed U.S. commissioners that they hoped to set foot on their new land before they should be asked to part with their old land.[7] The members of the Chickasaw delegation sent to explore the Choctaws' western lands in 1833 reported that the Choctaws were hostile to them. One of that party recounted that Choctaw warriors "trailed off their horses and then made them pay for their recovery, and they would hardly give a traveler a meal of victuals."[8] This unkindness could have reflected traditional clan enmity or may have been a show of Choctaw resistance to admitting the Chickasaw population to their new lands.

The letters of John Pitchlynn, a trader who had resided among the Choctaws since his youth, provide key information about pre–Indian Removal tensions between the Chickasaws and Choctaws. The Choctaws' official interpreter since 1782, Pitchlynn was an esteemed member of the nation, with more than a dozen children from two marriages to Choctaw women. Some of his sons received university educations and went on to become important Choctaw leaders.[9] While Pitchlynn remained in Mississippi (on Chickasaw lands), his eldest son by his second marriage, Peter, moved west with his family and his slaves.[10]

In a number of letters to Peter, Pitchlynn expressed concern that the Chickasaws would be relocated in the Choctaws' new home. "Some [Chickasaws] say they will go and live with the Choktaws and others say they will go the spanish country." The father worried about Chickasaw immigration, which, he warned, would bring indigent men as well as men of quality: "Some will be very rich and some as poor as dogs all the drunkards wil become hewers of timber and drawers of water to the white man."[11] He feared that Chickasaw immigrants would bring a flood of white traders to the Choctaws' new lands. They had intermarried more widely with whites, but Pitchlynn's main concern was that they would attract whiskey dealers.

As large Choctaw parties, which included some Chickasaws, journeyed to their new home, speculators and other white intruders overran the Chickasaws' Mississippi lands. The Chickasaws confronted thousands of non-Indian settlers who used every possible means to take control of their lands. Pitchlynn noted that whites purposely deluged the Chickasaws with "strong drink" to dispossess them. Presbyterian missionaries reported that there was very little drinking among the Chickasaws in 1829, but after Congress passed the Indian Removal Act, many drowned their sorrows in the bottle.[12] Pitchlynn observed, "There is more whisky drinking then ever was in the Chocktaws. I was at the last council there was more white man then Indians . . . and the[i]r object is to buy land."[13] Another witness to the sorrowful scene, Chickasaw agent Colonel Benjamin Reynolds, reported that "whiskey traders and peddlers—with other intruders upon the Indian land are over running the Country to the manifest injury of the Chickasaw tribe."[14] President Jackson encouraged Mississippians' corruption and false dealing.

Faced with destruction at the hands of white squatters, thieves, and whiskey traders, dozens of Chickasaws fled to the Choctaw Nation before any formal agreement was reached between the two nations. Pitchlynn noted with alarm in 1835 that soon the Chickasaws in Choctaw country would be "as thick as bees."[15] He shared the concern of many Choctaws that the Chickasaws would take their best lands before the Choctaws had their pick: "I say you must g[u]ard strong aga[i]ns[t] the Chickasaw coming if do not they will git all your good unsettled country."[16] He sounded this cautionary note because several Pitchlynn family members, like many Choctaw families, still remained in the East. In a number of letters, Pitchlynn asked his son to set aside land for his near relatives. "A great many of the Chickasaws start away next fall a great many to your country but you must not let them settel country that you lay off for mother and brothers and sisters you must mark it out this sumer."[17] Soon after Pitchlynn arrived in the Choctaws' new country, however, he became ill and died.

Like John Pitchlynn, Choctaw agent Captain William Armstrong saw the Chickasaws' coming as a drain on the Choctaws' resources, and he urged the Choctaw Council to reflect on future circumstances before finalizing plans to admit the Chickasaws to the Choctaw Nation. "You have yet a portion of your own people in the old nation that will come over and although you have a large country it is none too much and it should also be borne in mind that there is now no public lands."[18] While it is likely that many other Choctaws feared for the future, they probably also felt some degree of sympathy for the soon-to-be-homeless Chickasaws.

Neither the Chickasaws nor the Choctaws wanted to become one people, but their governments caved in to U.S. pressure. Jackson's secretary of war, John Eaton, was "fully sensible" that the Chickasaws were "unwilling to be merged in the tribe of the Choctaws," yet he planned to defeat the Chickasaw government's resistance.[19] Faced with Mississippians' invasion of their country, Chickasaw leaders petitioned Washington officials in 1836 to help them find a place where they could settle. After exhausting all other measures, anxious Chickasaw officials sought permission to live with the Choctaws. They petitioned President Jackson for U.S. assistance, stating that they "beheld their people without a home, surrounded by men whose language they can neither speak nor understand; subject to laws of which they are wholly ignorant, degraded, debased, and ruined."[20] Although the Choctaw Nation initially refused their request, Choctaw leaders finally relented and met with Chickasaw delegates at the Doaksville Convention of 1837 to work out an agreement.

The Chickasaw government empowered educated, bicultural chiefs James McLish, Pitman Colbert (Levi Colbert's nephew), James Brown, and James Perry to purchase land from the Choctaws. Its instructions to the delegates specified that the Chickasaw delegates were to secure land "free from all encumbrance or difficulty as to title."[21] However, the Choctaw government refused to sell lands outright. In the resulting treaty, the Chickasaw delegates did not obtain clear title to land. As a condition for admitting the Chickasaws into Choctaw country, Peter Pitchlynn, the principal Choctaw commissioner at Doaksville, demanded that the Chickasaws become Choctaw citizens. The Choctaw government assigned the Chickasaws their own political district, where the Chickasaws, constituting a majority, would elect their own representatives to the Choctaw Council. (Colonel Edmund Pickens was the first elected chief of the Chickasaw district and held this office until 1855.) The problem with this settlement was that the Choctaws assigned the Chickasaws lands that were nearly uninhabitable because western tribes already hunted there. When Choctaw leaders refused to make another offer, the Chickasaw delegates accepted the western region as their new home and consented to political unification.[22]

Levi Colbert had once questioned whether submission to Choctaw leaders would be more agreeable than submission to Mississippi's state laws; however, the Chickasaw delegates, with no clear alternative, signed away the Chickasaw government's political and judicial autonomy at Doaksville in 1837. Americans were the main beneficiaries of the arrangement, for it deflected the Chickasaws' resentment from Mississippi and the U.S. government to the Choctaw government.

After removing to Indian Territory, Chickasaw immigrants declared that they had not realized that they would have to submit to Choctaw laws and governance—that this was not well understood. They had commissioned their delegates to purchase their own lands in the Choctaws' territory. Instead, they learned that for $530,000 the delegates had consented to an arrangement that stripped them of their laws and government, just as the state of Mississippi had done. They complained that the Doaksville Treaty made them "subordinate to the Choctaw government, a government utterly foreign to their habits and offensive to their national pride."[23] They refused to accept all the arrangements and conditions to which their representatives had agreed in the treaty.

After relocation, the Chickasaws still lacked a secure and habitable place to rebuild their clan-based communities. They feared the western tribes and found that their assigned district lacked open roads and mountain passes.[24] Furthermore, the Chickasaws' acting agent, Gaines P. Kingsbury, said that it would be impracticable to supply them in their isolated territory and insisted that they get provisions from trading depots in the Choctaw Nation.[25] Kingsbury did not want to have to defend the western frontier or to pay a separate agent for the Chickasaws. Concerned about expenditures, he encouraged the Chickasaws to "settle promiscuously with the Choctaw" in the eastern division of their lands in Indian Territory.[26] The Choctaw agent, Armstrong, reported in 1838 that only about a dozen Chickasaw families had risked settling in their district.[27]

Weakened by dysentery, malnutrition, and smallpox, many Chickasaws were stalled in immigrant camps for long periods of time. They depended on the substandard rations doled out at supply depots. Conditions at the five immigrant stations were deplorable, and over five hundred Chickasaws died there of disease.[28] Exploited by merchants, the immigrants became indebted and quickly lost their horses, cattle, and other property. Major General Ethan Allen Hitchcock reported to Washington in 1841: "Creditors are gradually stripping the thoughtless of everything which constitutes an Indians' wealth; even . . . to their very rifles in some instances."[29] Angered that whites had taken their homelands and subjected them to spoiled rations, some Chickasaws wanted to reject American-style dress and farming and return to the old ways. With forests teeming with game, some Chickasaws returned to the hunt and resumed an independent subsistence lifestyle. They moved out to the woodlands in the northern portion of the Choctaw Nation, where they rebuilt their homes in secluded spots, far from roads carrying white travelers and traders.

Intent on merging the two peoples, Kingsbury failed to report the lingering tensions between the Chickasaws and the Choctaws, who resented the newcomers' presence and called them "intruders." The Chickasaws noted in discussions with Major Hitchcock that it was "frequently thrown up to them as a reproach that they have no right in the country."[30] Most Chickasaws were dissatisfied; they could be found "continually breaking up their homes and seeking new locations." They expected to move in a short time to their own district, and consequently, only a small number of them established permanent homesteads in eastern Choctaw country. This group of wealthy Chickasaws settled in the southern region of the Choctaw Nation and built their plantations along waterways and wagon routes.[31]

As the Chickasaws regrouped in their assigned district, they resented the Choctaw Nation's laws directing their affairs and defended their own ancient customs. They rebelled against certain Choctaw laws that seemed like "white man's laws," declaring that they did "not like whites or their ways or anything in imitation of them."[32] Choctaw observers noted that the Chickasaws continued the "old customs more generally and many of them have several wives," even though the Choctaw Constitution prohibited this custom.[33] Malcolm McGee, a white interpreter for the Chickasaws, recalled, "The majority [of men] in the nation [seemed] content with one wife; some, however, had two and even more. One doctor I knew had seven wives, all living in separate lodges."[34] Even after the Civil War, several Chickasaws still practiced polygamy; whenever brought to trial, they requested a Chickasaw jury, which usually judged them innocent of committing a crime. Levi Colbert's adopted son Winchester Colbert was tried in 1869 in a Chickasaw court for having multiple wives. He admitted practicing polygamy but denied that it was an unlawful activity (and was released without a fine).[35] In fact, the Chickasaw legislature outlawed polygamy in 1857, but the law was not strictly enforced.[36]

Prior to Indian Removal, the Chickasaws had had far less contact than the Choctaws with missionaries; none followed them to the West or established churches in the Chickasaw district. In the 1830s some Chickasaw leaders, such as George Colbert, had discouraged missionaries, stating that they did not want to get their people all "screwed up" like the Choctaws. Colbert mocked the missionaries' camp meetings as nothing but "jumping, hallowing, [and] crying."[37] If there was any change, hardships in Indian Territory had made traditional Chickasaws even more hostile to missionaries and Christian schools. Principal hereditary chief Minko Ishtehotopa opposed them altogether. In describing many Chickasaws' strong allegiance to Minko Ishtehotopa (d. 1848), Agent A. M. M. Upshaw alluded to the Chickasaw people's "prejudices in favor of the old Indian customs." Upshaw decried Ishtehotopa's influence, maintaining that he was uneducated and opposed missionary schools in part because the missionaries were hostile to him.[38]

The Chickasaw Commission, which had continued as the de facto government, ruled that annuity payments would go only to tribal members whose Chickasaw blood came from their mother's side. This showed the commission's determination to stick to the "old ways" and perhaps an attempt to restrict the distribution of national funds to a smaller group. Sloan Love, a wealthy Chickasaw who built a horse-drawn corn mill and cotton gin in the Chickasaw district, maintained that traditionally all rights to national lands were derived through the mother and he intended access to national funds to be similarly determined: "Thus a Chickasaw marrying a Choctaw woman would retain his own right during life, but his children have no claim. A Choctaw, marrying a Chickasaw woman, the woman would enjoy her right and her children would inherit it."[39] Love had his way, as the Chickasaw agent reported in 1843: "The rule that the Chickasaw have adopted is to leave out a great number that lived with them in the old nation and all those who have married amongst them, whose mother is not a Chickasaw."[40] As late as 1878, Chickasaw delegates argued that the mother is exclusively charged with "the support and nurture of the children . . . [that the children] do not inherit the property of the father . . . [and that] descent even in the cases of their kings are always traced through the maternal line."[41] This insistence on matrilineal inheritance put them at odds with the Choctaws, whose Constitution of 1826 established laws protecting the rights of inheritance through the male line.[42]

Some of the tribe sought a revival of the traditional government led by Minko Ishtehotopa and other hereditary chiefs. Upshaw sided with the faction of the tribe—the wealthier, more educated Chickasaws—that leaned toward the election of public officials. In 1845 to preserve unity, the members of the Chickasaw Commission resigned. Chickasaws who supported a return to hereditary government yielded to those who favored tribal elections. Opposition to the Choctaws helped to unify the two groups. Initially, slave-holding planters were more accepting of the new political arrangements. They left the immigrant stations behind and focused their efforts on building their plantations and grooming their children for political office.[43] However, conflicts over financial matters, and the interpretation of wills and the transfer of slaves and other property, led even the most commercially oriented planters to resent Choctaw dominance in politics and the courts.

Financial jealousies made the Chickasaws and Choctaws distrustful of each other. U.S. commissioners had led the Choctaws to believe that in time they would share equally in the Chickasaws' resources and that the addition of the Chickasaws' national funds and population would make the Choctaws a great nation. The Chickasaws had received more money for their homeland and had larger per capita annuities. The Doaksville Convention of 1837 acknowledged the Chickasaws' right to elect their own officials, who retained exclusive control over their national funds. Looking back at the problems they created, U.S. officials noted that this stipulation was "calculated to perpetuate and keep alive their national distinctions."[44]

Financial matters were a continual sore spot between the tribes. In 1847 Peter Pitchlynn brought a $5,000 claim against the Chickasaw government, based on the fact that the Chickasaws had paid part of the stipulated $530,000 agreed upon at Doaksville in bonds, not cash. Pitchlynn's victory in the suit contributed to ill feelings between the tribes. The Chickasaws complained that they had to bear the administrative expenses of their own district and that they benefited little from the money paid to the Choctaw government in 1837.[45] Mutual antagonism caused the Chickasaws to draw territorial and ethnic boundaries between themselves and the Choctaws.

Although most Chickasaws resided outside of the Chickasaw district for at least a decade, they refused to spend any of their national funds to improve lands in the eastern portion of the Choctaw Nation, saving the money for the time when they could build and foster permanent institutions in their own section. The Chickasaws regarded their assigned district more as an independent state than as part of the Choctaw Nation, and they wanted its boundaries clearly marked so that any school buildings or homes they erected fell on their side of the line. The U.S. agent to the Choctaws, Douglas Cooper, noted, "The Chickasaws being the weaker tribe, are naturally afraid the Choctaws will acquire the preponderance by settlement" in the Chickasaw district.[46] No one had an accurate map of the Choctaw Nation's land, for the exact placement of boundaries had seemed inconsequential in 1837. Now Chickasaw and Choctaw neighbors disputed a margin of about twenty miles. Cooper estimated that by strict adherence to the terms of the Doaksville Convention, nearly two-thirds of the Choctaw Nation was assigned as the Chickasaw district.[47] The Choctaws resented the Chickasaws' attempt to reserve these vast lands for themselves, and worried that they had built homes in the Chickasaw district. If their farms fell on the wrong side of the line when it was finally drawn, they would "be ruined and driven from their homes."[48] Jacob Folsom, a Choctaw district representative, recounted that when Sloan Love demanded in 1841 that the Chickasaw district's eastern boundary be settled, the other members of the Choctaw Council "went against heavily and tore him to tatters. . . . They say it was a poor speech he made." As a result of his mistreatment, Love flew into a "maniac" rage, and the Choctaw light-horsemen (tribal police) took him away and confined him to the military garrison.[49] Although Folsom questioned Love's sanity, the Chickasaws continued to hold him in high regard and in 1844 appointed him one of their commissioners in charge of distributing tribal funds. As tensions reached a boiling point, the Chickasaws found it necessary to appeal to the United States to resolve their boundary dispute with the Choctaws.

To the Choctaws, the Chickasaws' preoccupation with boundaries reflected their unwillingness to contribute to the greater good of the Choctaw Nation, of which they were now a part. Most obviously, the Chickasaws were unwilling to cooperate on improvements, such as schools and churches, that might benefit both peoples.[50] Though a much smaller nation, the Chickasaws put aside $10,000 annually for their children's education, whereas the Choctaws reserved only $6,000 for that purpose. The Chickasaws wanted to use their school funds for their own national good.[51]

Missionaries failed to break down the Chickasaws' national sentiment or to recognize their legitimate concerns. Missionary James S. Allen expressed annoyance at Chickasaw leaders' urgent request to locate Wapanucka Academy "within their own bounds." Allen asserted that the boundary between the nations was merely an "imaginary one" and that the purpose of the government was to unify the two peoples. By treaty right, the Chickasaws had no more title to the lands in the Chickasaw district than they had to lands elsewhere in the Choctaw Nation. But in the early 1850s the Chickasaws were looking ahead to the time when their people would be reunited in their own district, and they feared the complications that would result when they tried to assert control over Wapanucka Academy if it landed on the Choctaws' side of the boundary line. They confided that they "had no faith in their Choktaw brethren" and saw that it landed west of the Choctaw-Chickasaw boundary.[52]

An outgrowth of the boundary dispute was judicial conflict. The uncertain boundary gave "rise to conflict of jurisdiction" because the

Chickasaws contended that they received unfair trials before Choctaw judges and juries.[53] When a Chickasaw was convicted of murder, the verdict reached by the "court composed entirely of Choctaws" was "life for life." If a Choctaw had committed the murder, that rule was "generally suspended." Choctaw light-horsemen sometimes came into the Chickasaw district unannounced and took Chickasaw property, explaining to the owners that a Choctaw judge had authorized them to do so. Inheritance disputes arose because the Chickasaws and Choctaws had intermarried extensively, and the settlement of estates inflamed the jurisdictional battle. Angry Chickasaw claimants took slaves and horses back by force. Territorial and judicial disputes occasionally ended "in the death of one or another of the parties and the number of these are constantly increasing."[54] In one incident that caused a great deal of tension between the tribes, district chief Edmund Pickens's son David, acting as a Chickasaw light-horseman, killed a Choctaw bootlegger carrying liquor across the Red River from north Texas.[55]

The Chickasaws sent a delegation to Washington in 1848 to lobby for their own distinct territory and independent government. Minko Ishtehotopa had died, and Chickasaw leaders like Pickens, Winchester Colbert, and Cyrus Harris advocated constitutional government. They tied this aspiration to the goal pursued by their people—independence from the Choctaw government. Officials noted that the Chickasaw delegates to Washington "wish[ed] to get a country for themselves."[56] When the delegation returned to Indian Territory, the Chickasaw agent counseled its members to put aside all ideas of independence. He insisted that separation was "impracticable" and financially unobtainable.[57] But the Chickasaws longed for their political freedom. Intermarried Chickasaw William Guy tired of hearing people say that the "Chickasaws were incapacitated for self-government, that the Choctaws could govern the Chickasaws better than they could govern themselves which is a gross absurdity."[58]

In the 1850s the Chickasaws hired lawyers and lobbyists to advance their cause in Washington. Their complaints, particularly the charge that the Choctaw government was tyrannical, angered the indignant Choctaws. The Chickasaws claimed self-determination as a natural right, comparing themselves to the American patriots of 1776. They held that "when a government becomes unable to sustain itself, and fails to give that protection due to whom she governs, she at once ceases to be a government."[59] The Chickasaws maintained that their present political connection was "destructive of their rights, liberty, and happiness as a people," adding that "these principles are as dear to the red man as to the whites, to the Chickasaws as to the American citizens."[60] They claimed that they were prepared to take up arms against the Choctaw Nation, for Americans had themselves shown that the "inalienable right of revolution exists." Here the Chickasaws used the rhetoric embodied in the American Declaration of Independence to regain their autonomy as an Indian nation. The Choctaws complained that their side of the story was not heard because they spent less money than the Chickasaws on lobbyists: "If we had plenty money we should never be held out to the world that we were oppressive upon the Chickasaws."[61]

The Chickasaws in the 1850s operated from a position of greater strength than they had in 1837. They were secure in possession of their homes, and they staged a moving rally in 1853 to show that they were unified in their quest for political sovereignty. Chickasaw agent Andrew Smith recorded the event with admiration: "The tall and manly looking old chief Col. [Edmund] Pickens marching off in front and the warriors following in single file to the distance of about a quarter of a mile whence they turned forming an oval at the juncture they stopped to see who and how many were on the other side of the question when they found none—the vote being unanimous for an Independent government." Agent Smith counted over four hundred warriors in the line trailing district chief Pickens.[62] The circular style of this parade was reminiscent of the Chickasaws' hunting and war formations, as described by trader Thomas Nairne in the early eighteenth century.[63] The Chickasaw Nation staged this ceremonial march to silence enemies who alleged that it was divided on the issue of seeking independence from the Choctaws and to publicize its resolution to the wider world.[64]

In 1852 Thomas Pitchlynn reported on the Chickasaws' state building. He heard that the Chickasaws had moved their council house ten miles west on Pennington Creek and "appropriated one hundred thousand dollars to b[u]ild a national house, chiefs house &c. this was done a few days since."[65] Although settled, unified, and engaged in the construction of their own national buildings, the Chickasaws still had to overcome Choctaw opposition to their political separation. The Doaksville Treaty was a legal document approved by the commissioner of Indian affairs and sanctioned by President Martin Van Buren. It had legally stripped the Chickasaws' of their national and political character. Even the Chickasaws' friends in Washington recognized that the Choctaws' interpretation of the treaty was sound and that the Choctaws had fulfilled all the obligations imposed upon them. Placed on the defensive, the majority of Choctaws opposed Chickasaw independence. The Chickasaws' charges stained their honor, and they looked upon Chickasaw secession as a sacrifice of their national interests. Choctaw leaders insisted, "We cannot consent to the sale or alienation beyond our own ultimate control of one foot of our country."[66] Without U.S. aid and some Choctaw support, the Chickasaws could not compel the Choctaw Nation to negotiate.

A minority of the Choctaws welcomed separation because they calculated that the Chickasaws were willing to pay a large sum to regain their independence. Choctaw J. Wall wrote, "I think they will want a treaty with the Choctaws before long if they do than that will be the time for the Choctaws to make their fortune if they only will be smart . . . we are broke of revenue and want one and now is the time to make it of them." Wall pointed out that the Chickasaws hoarded their national funds and did not contribute materially to the Choctaws' educational institutions: "They are a drag to the Choctaws plainly speaking they are no advantage to us as they will not partake or take an active part with us [the Choctaws] in the encouragement of civilization—so what do we want with such people."[67] Thomas Pitchlynn, brother to Peter, saw the separation as inevitable and pointless to resist: "The Chickasaws are determine[d] to have their district and if the Choctaws do not agree to their propersisions [propositions] they will declare their Independence and receive the same fate." Pitchlynn noted that the Hungarians had recently attained their independence from Austria and he did not see what would block the Chickasaws from gaining theirs.[68] Peter Pitchlynn allegedly accepted money from the Chickasaw Nation to secure his backing for independence. The Choctaw Nation used the Chickasaw issue as leverage in its claims cases against the federal government, which grew out of Indian Removal policy inequities during the 1830s and nonfulfillment of treaty obligations.[69]

Finally, the Chickasaws' arguments, the federal government's desire to relocate the Comanches on Chickasaw and Choctaw lands, and the threat of a major war in Indian Territory convinced the U.S. government that a different arrangement between the tribes was warranted.[70] Policy makers admitted that the policy of merging smaller tribes with larger ones had become a disaster. In 1854 the year before the Chickasaws won their political independence, the Chickasaw agent wrote, "The few remaining difficulties and subjects of dissatisfaction existing among the tribes of the superintendence grow out . . . of the previous policy of the government of forcing upon weak tribes an unnatural union with stronger ones." He concluded that "the separation must take place—there can be no peace without it."[71]

Ultimately, difficult relations between the two tribes were resolved when the Chickasaws proposed a representative government that gained legitimacy in the eyes of the U.S. government. The United States was receptive to the Chickasaws' appeals for autonomy because it wanted to bring the tribes back to the negotiating table for more land cessions. The Treaty of 1855, to which the United States was a third party, empowered the Chickasaws to create a sovereign nation. The Chickasaws' victory was limited, however. The Choctaws refused to grant the Chickasaws unencumbered title to their assigned district, and future land cessions and U.S. treaties as well as contracts with railroads, mining operations, and ranch outfits would entail both nations' consent.[72]

The Chickasaw Nation adopted a constitution based on the U.S. Constitution on August 30, 1856, that established its nation as separate from the Choctaws. The Chickasaws likewise commemorated their last war chief by establishing a capital named Tishomingo after the beloved warrior who had died during migration to Indian Territory. Whether Chickasaws attended pashofa dances and funeral cries, or continued to speak the Chickasaw language, were now measures of individual identity, not citizenship. The Chickasaws were citizens of the Chickasaw Nation under its new constitution and laws, which codified the Chickasaws' political sovereignty and exclusionary policies. They stripped from the Choctaw residents of the Chickasaw district the right to vote or to serve in the Chickasaw government. The Chickasaws justified their policy of disfranchisement by arguing that if enough Choctaw people settled within their country, they could control their elections, and thus tribal revenues and finances.[73] The Chickasaws also enacted legislation to deny Choctaw children access to their schools.

Although the Chickasaws and Choctaws had much in common, the attempted absorption of the Chickasaw people into the Choctaw Nation had eroded long-standing cultural bonds and sympathies. Intermarriages had been occurring between the Chickasaws and Choctaws for decades, yet kinship ties did not replace or serve as substitutes for individuals' national allegiance and pride. The Chickasaws regained their name and political power, and reserved their wealth to promote the success of their own people.

The Chickasaws' political struggle against the Choctaws was but one example of the unsuccessful U.S. policy of forcing historically separate Indian tribes to live together and participate in a single territorial government. Other such examples include the Seminoles' opposition to amalgamation with the Creeks and the conflict between the Five Tribes and the western Indians who occupied Indian Territory and the forced merger of the Delawares from Kansas with the Cherokees. Whites involved in determining policy regarding the Indians, and particularly Indian Removal policy, failed to understand the Indians' perspectives, the relationships among the tribes, and the pride with which Indians viewed membership in their particular tribe.

2

Trouble with Texans and Western Indians, 1830s–1890s

Chickasaw identity, as distinct from that of the western tribes, was a key to their landholding, autonomy, and favored status as one of the Five Civilized Tribes. In the nineteenth century, American policy makers categorized the Indian occupants of present-day Oklahoma and Texas as the "wild" Indians and the Chickasaws and other southeastern Indian immigrants as the "civilized" tribes. The Chickasaws moved into the hunting grounds of dislocated Indian tribes from regions north and west of Oklahoma such as the Comanches, Osages, Caddos, and Kickapoos. In the view of the federal government, the Chickasaws were one step ahead of these Indians in the racial hierarchy because they were literate, had intermarried with whites, and were partially Christianized. This was the cultural context in which, during much of the nineteenth century, the Chickasaws struggled for security and autonomy against the western tribes, white Texans, and the U.S. government. Forced onto western Indians' lands by the federal government and bordered by dangerous, Indian-hating Texas neighbors, the Chickasaws hardened their definition of themselves, as different from and superior to the western Indians.

From 1826, when the Chickasaws first entered into talks with the U.S. government about their relocation to Indian Territory, they emphasized their progress toward the American definition of civilization: they had largely given up the hunt, and become farmers and even, in some cases, prosperous cotton planters. They no longer warred against other Indians, unless in the service of the U.S. Army, and they claimed educations from fine Indian neighborhood and boarding schools that rivaled those in the States.

The Chickasaws were attached to their homeland by history and solemn promises to their ancestors to safeguard the lands that past warriors had defended with their lives. Referring to such ties won little sympathy from Americans, so Chickasaw leaders emphasized instead that their relocation might compromise their educational achievements—in white terms, their progress toward civilization. They did not want to move to a wilderness, where conflict with the "warlike tribes" might obstruct their efforts toward self-improvement. They could not unite with the Indians of the West as one people—it would be as hard as combining oil and water. Chickasaw chief Levi Colbert wrote President Andrew Jackson, "In one minute you can see the strong and marked difference of our condition here and in the wild distant regions of the west surrounded by none but distant and dear trade and warlike tribes thrown together, these are some of the evils."[1]

The Chickasaws had unsettled scores with the Osages and other warriors who had resisted their intrusion into their hunting grounds in Arkansas, Louisiana, and Texas Territory. In the 1790s Chickasaw volunteers had fought against the Kickapoos on behalf of the United States and now they imagined that "those tribes will take satisfaction of us for injuries done by us as well as our white brothers."[2] Moreover, they knew that their relocation to the western Indians' hunting grounds would provoke new conflicts. They wanted to stay in their Mississippi homeland, where they were free of their "Red enemies," for renewed warfare against the western Indians could destroy their small nation.[3]

Another concern of the Chickasaws was that by sharing the same lands as western Indians, they would be relegated to the inferior status of a "wild tribe." As one of the Five Tribes, the Chickasaws had treaty guarantees acknowledging their right to self-governance that the less favored Indians lacked, and they also had U.S. Indian agents in their lands to present their grievances to the secretary of the interior. Addressing the Chickasaws' anxiety about being relegated to a lower status, Commissioner General John Coffee assured them that the president regarded them with the same affection he felt for his "white children."[4] With equal insincerity, President Andrew Jackson promised to guard the Chickasaws from enemies of every kind, whether "white or red." The Chickasaws may not have known it then, but hostile Texans would prove as menacing as hostile Comanches.[5]

U.S. officials knew that Chickasaw immigrants were entering a dangerous situation in Indian Territory, but they were not as committed as they claimed to providing them with adequate protection. In 1835 U.S. commissioners mediated a peace between the western Indians and groups of eastern Indians who had already settled in Indian Territory.[6] It was a halfhearted effort. Superintendent of Indian Affairs for the Western Territory Major Francis W. Armstrong admitted that the talks did not go well: "Our means for presents and for the expenses of the Treaty, being extremely limited, we only gave them a small quantity of Tobacco, to conciliate their good feelings." He added that many "Warriors expressed a perfect indifference as to the success of the Treaty" because they profited from horse theft and enjoyed control over the hunting grounds in question.[7] Indeed, the Comanches and other Indians protested their meager gifts, which totaled only $300, hardly a decent recompense for welcoming Indian newcomers who would kill off or drive away their game.[8] When western Indians attacked immigrant parties of the Five Tribes, U.S. officials were unwilling to take responsibility for them, alleging that Mexican agents had instigated the raids.[9]

Of all the Five Tribes, the Chickasaws were the most exposed to the raids of the displaced and unsettled Indian bands in Indian Territory.[10] The Chickasaws' new homeland was bordered and inhabited by several bands of western Indians. Shawnees, Delawares, and Kickapoos lived along the Canadian River, and Comanches and Osages hunted in the vicinity of the Red River. A Chickasaw settler recalled, "The Choctaws gave the western part of the land allotted them to the Chickasaws, because they were afraid of the Comanches who were their neighbors on the West."[11]

Almost as soon as the Chickasaws arrived in the Choctaw Nation, the Indian agent in Indian Territory reneged on President Jackson's guarantee of protection. Agent Gaines P. Kingsbury in 1837 argued that the country was too isolated for his limited military forces to protect.[12] He advised the Chickasaws against moving into their assigned district. Removal agent R. D. Collins concurred, stating that the Chickasaws could not settle in their own district without losing all their horses to the "wild Indians," if not experiencing greater misfortunes.[13] The Chickasaws who dismissed Kingsbury's and Collins's warnings and moved into the region faced repeated raids. Kingsbury observed: "The Chickasaws have a great many horses and considerable property. Unless those scattering bands are removed, the property of the Chickasaws will be in danger as well as their advancement greatly retarded." The Chickasaws had already "lost a considerable quantity of stock and live constantly in fear of losing more. Parties of friendly Indians come in daily, complaining of depredations being committed on them by the wild Indians."[14]

The Paul family, who settled in the western district before the United States built forts there for the Chickasaws' protection, learned to live in peace with most of the western Indians who frequented the region. The Pauls were friendly and extended hospitality to them. As William Paul remembered his grandfather Smith Paul stating: "The 'horse riding' Indians were always hungry, so if you fed them 'til they're full, they would never hurt you."[15] With the buffalo gone and their hunting grounds compromised, the Kickapoos, Comanches, and other western tribes survived by raiding the Texans', Choctaws', and Chickasaws' farms. In addition to their theft of horses, they carried on a brisk trade in African slaves and white captives. Joseph Robertson, an intermarried white Chickasaw, petitioned the U.S. government for intervention in April 1841 to retrieve two slaves whom the Comanches had stolen for ransom. He denied that the western Indians were vengeful or influenced by Mexicans. They undertook their raids simply for "the sake of plunder."[16]

When the Chickasaws arrived in Indian Territory, they stepped into the charged environment of Texas-Indian wars. To Texans, Indians of any name were potential conspirators with Mexico in its fight against Texas. But even after the United States annexed Texas in 1846, Texans remained hostile toward the Indians in their midst. As Captain Randolph B. Marcy of the U.S. Army explained, the old problems the Indians faced had not changed: "The borderers of Texas have often made war upon [the Indians] without the slightest provocation, and have, time and time again, robbed them of their fields, and forced them to abandon their agricultural improvements, and remove farther and farther away. . . . They have been robbed, murdered, and starved, until they have been reduced to mere skeletons of nominal tribes."[17]

Texans forced Indian bands out of their republic in the late 1830s and into the Chickasaws' assigned district. Texas legislators reportedly told a Kickapoo chief that "there was a fine country over here on the Washita and plenty of game, that red men lived there who were good men and could give him and his people land to reside upon and that he advised him and his people to go over there and settle."[18] Driven from Texas, Kickapoo leaders begged the Chickasaw leaders for shelter and hunting rights. In 1839 one Kickapoo chief said that "his people were nearly starving and he wished to get a country where he could find game to hunt and raise a little corn to keep his people from starving."[19] He urged them to remember that they were Indians, too, and therefore should understand the principle of holding lands in common. Kingsbury paraphrased his speech: "The red people were all brothers and . . . they ought to suffer each other he thought to travel through their different countries. He knew that the great America chief had divided that Country into little strips for the different tribes, but he thought they ought to have one country and go where they chose. He said that there was but one Great Spirit and that he had made all this country."[20] Though the members of the Chickasaw Council smoked tobacco with the Kickapoo chief as a token of peace, they denied his request "to plant corn." Alarmed at warring between Kickapoos and Osages within the Chickasaw district, and potential violence between Kickapoos and Texans, the council petitioned the commissioner of Indian Affairs to remove the invaders. Kingsbury informed the Kickapoos that the Chickasaws "wanted this country for themselves and did not wish any other Indians to settle in it."[21] The Chickasaws stated that if the Indian claimants had "any right (which we deny) to the country, we hold that the United States is bound to extinguish that right in our favor."[22]

Chickasaw delegates headed to Washington to urge the U.S. government to drive western Indians from their lands. They came armed with the U.S. treaty guarantee "to drive all those persons that were living and occupying our country, beyond our limits. Now it is right, it is just, that the United States should deliver to us our country free from molestation."[23] The United States was obligated to provide them with a secure new home. For security of persons and property, and out of indignation arising from the most recent violation of their treaty guarantees, the Chickasaws wanted their assigned district to be their own land exclusively.[24]

Although they did not welcome the Kickapoos, the Chickasaws never regarded all the scattered Indian bands as equally threatening to them. In 1853 the Chickasaw chiefs agreed to shelter bands of Delaware Indians, recently driven from Texas in the middle of winter. They were moved by the Delawares' predicament, perhaps likening it to their own experience of forced removal. The Delawares said that they wanted to rest in the Chickasaw Nation until spring, for their trek to a distant reserve in Indian Territory would endanger their women and children and also destroy a large quantity of their cattle due to exposure. The Chickasaw chiefs offered them "the privilege to settle in our District subject to our laws and all the privileges and penalties thereof."[25] By 1857, the Delawares had overstayed their welcome through their too close association with the Comanche trade in white captives and livestock from Texas, and the Chickasaw legislature passed a resolution that ordered the Delawares "roaming through and infesting that portion of the Choctaw Nation known as the Chickasaw District" to leave. Soon the Delawares would be settled permanently among the Cherokees.[26]

Chickasaws suffered repeated invasion of their country by Texans in pursuit of western Indian raiders. General Ethan Allen Hitchcock observed in 1842 that "armed Texans have crossed Red river and committed acts of violence that have alarmed the quiet and peaceable Choctaws & Chickasaws."[27] When Texas Rangers resolved to exterminate the "wild" bands who "knew not God," they called upon Chickasaw warriors for assistance to put the western Indians "to the sword."[28] The Chickasaws, not trusting the Texans, sent delegates to Washington, D.C., to seek advice and military assistance (mostly against the Texans).[29]

Few Texans cared to distinguish between friendly and hostile Indians, and they considered anyone selling arms to their Comanche enemies to be enemies of Texas. When Chickasaw chief George Colbert led a trading expedition to a Comanche camp located on the Chickasaw-Texas border, a company of Texas Rangers warned him out of the republic.[30] Texans maintained that if the Chickasaws "have not been actually engaged in the depredations, now being continually carried on by Indians upon our frontier (which is the prevalent opinion here)," they gave "them every aid assistance and protection in their power." Texan militia leaders held them responsible for "affording an asylum" to marauding Indians.[31] In other words, the Chickasaws were guilty by association with their Comanche neighbors.

In one instance, a party of Texans followed a Chickasaw across the Red River and killed him in his own land. Texans asserted that they had been pursuing a band of Couchatta Indians who were at war with Texas and believed that they had killed a member of that hostile group.[32] In 1848 Texas Rangers clashed with a party of Waco Indians in the vicinity of Fort Washita, killing twelve. The continued presence of the Rangers was unsettling to the Chickasaws.[33] It is no wonder that they asked Hitchcock to appeal to the United States for protection from the Texans in particular.[34]

It was true that some Chickasaws engaged in an arms trade with the western bands for stolen property, including the ransom of white captives. Hitchcock noted that "powder is sold to those tribes by traders from our side of mixed blood, prisoners bought."[35] In 1840 Chickasaw Ishtekahtubby, who was not a "mixed blood," went on a trading expedition to the Comanches and purchased a white captive. He offered to go back and get other prisoners but wanted to know first "what would he get for it."[36] Ishtekahtubby was a hereditary chief, indicating that prominent Chickasaws engaged in this profitable business. Chickasaw Aaron Brown and his trading partner, Kickapoo Johnson, turned over two white boys, captives of the Comanches, to a U.S. officer in expectation of remuneration. Brown and Johnson received nearly $1,000 compensation for their trouble and the expense of retrieving the Wilson boys.[37]

Some Chickasaw traders may have actually encouraged the Texans' conflict with the western Indians. In 1847 U.S. Indian commissioner Robert Neighbors wrote that traders from the eastern Indian nations "found it much to their interest to keep those wild bands hostile, as their plunder offered a profitable source of traffic." Neighbors held that the western Indians "were very credulous and liable at all times to be led astray by their more civilized neighbors, especially when it is to the interest of those bands to create disaffection." He said that a group of eastern Indians reportedly told the Comanches "that the whites were preparing to wage a war of extermination on the Indians; that the government would not comply with its promises."[38]

For their part, several Texans were engaged in robbing the Chickasaws' horses and slaves, and cheating them out of their property through liquor sales. Overton Love and John Guest of the Chickasaw Nation sought legal redress for slaves stolen by whites from Texas.[39] The state of lawlessness on the Chickasaw-frontier border encouraged renegade white Texans to take advantage of the situation. Often dressed as Indians, they stole cattle and horses at will, knowing where the blame would fall.

The Texas Rangers' aggressive anti-Indian campaigns made it imperative that the Chickasaws promote themselves as friendly, "civilized" Indians and distance themselves from the Delawares, who acted as the primary middlemen in the illicit Comanche trade. U.S. Indian inspector William J. Pollock observed that "the aggressive frontiersmen, struggling continually for the Indians' lands, continually misrepresent them." Despite what the Texans made them out to be, Inspector Pollock asserted that the Indians of the Five Tribes were "not wild untutored savages . . . but in fact as in name self-supporting, self-governing, civilized people."[40] The explorer Josiah Gregg acknowledged the Choctaws and Chickasaws as "the most quiet and Christian-like Indians of the Texas border."[41]

In another instance, the Chickasaw government welcomed a party of Shawnees, who were peaceful farmers. White observers noted that the Shawnee residents of the Chickasaw Nation showed "proofs of rapid advancement in civilization . . . an abundance of provisions, corn, etc."[42] In 1859 the Chickasaw legislature adopted "George Washington and his Shawnee warriors comprising 168 persons in all." They rewarded Shawnee chief Washington for performing a valuable service: he sent reports to Chickasaw governors informing them of the latest Comanche attacks on the frontier.[43] These Shawnees could remain in the nation subject to its laws, but although "adopted," they could not partake of the Chickasaw annuity or national funds.[44] They eventually joined other Shawnees on lands set aside for them in the Cherokee Nation.

The potential for cultural conflict between the Chickasaws and western Indians was heightened by the fact that the group of Chickasaws that had the most direct contact with the Comanches were the most acculturated of their nation—the wealthiest property owners, as well as the most literate. They were very different from the western Indians who hunted in their newly assigned home. Although the great majority of Chickasaws lived simply, as semisubsistence farmers in "cabins of logs like those of our backwoods settlers," some Chickasaw planters lived in the fashion of the southern elite.[45] Gregg observed that the "wealthier class" of Chickasaws had "adopted substantially the Southern system of slavery," and Chickasaw planters lived on the same scale and shared the same lifestyle as the surrounding white planter class.[46]

It was these planters and intermarried whites and their Chickasaw families who first moved to the region that was claimed and occupied by the western Indians and other dislocated bands. To graze their numerous horses and livestock, they needed to occupy more land than remained in the settled sections of Indian Territory. Moreover, they used slave labor and white hired hands to bring many acres of land into cultivation with a view to the developing markets in cotton, animal feed, and food for white travelers.

In 1842 the U.S. government established Fort Washita in response to the Chickasaws' and Texans' repeated requests for security against Comanche raids. The fort immediately became a trading center for the western bands and provided a market for Chickasaw planters' produce. The Chickasaw agent reported in 1849 that "there are more of the various tribes of Indians passing to and fro in the vicinity of this post than any other post, perhaps, in the United States." Hitchcock noted, "The peltries sent in by the traders mostly come from either the wild Indians or the Shawnees."[47]

To the western Indians, the fort was both welcome and feared. The Indians did not fear the soldiers, who were not even mounted on horses, but they feared the growing presence of Indian planters, intermarried whites, and travelers and their effect on dwindling game, forests, and grasses. American emigrants headed for Texas, New Mexico, and California gathered at encampments near Fort Washita to await fellow travelers before starting on the more dangerous portion of their trip. Some enterprising Chickasaw planters took advantage of the traffic though their lands. They provided corn and fodder at high prices. The Chickasaw agent remarked that the Chickasaw families "situated from within 10 or 20 miles of the fort furnish it with butter, potatoes, chicken, eggs, etc." To please their white guests, planters kept their smokehouses "filled with meat, lard, and molasses."[48]

Numerous white travelers commented with surprise at how well middling Chickasaws lived in this mostly wild frontier. Fort Washita private John Whaley described the Indian settlements surrounding the fort: "The inhabitants are hard to describe. The greater part of them are a mixture of the white man and the Indian. You will see once and while a man from the states . . . who have married squaws."[49] Virtually the entire Love family settled on the Red River below Fort Washita, a region later named Love Valley. Isaac Love's two-story frame house had a gallery and parlor filled with "red plush furniture." Isaac was one of several children of English slaveholder Thomas Love and Chickasaw Sally Colbert. At widow Sara McLish Colbert's home, visitors found a private room, "a good bed . . . with clean neat bed clothes, white pillow cases, ruffled."[50] Most of the men and women with Love and Colbert surnames adopted planter lifestyles that differentiated them from most Chickasaws—and certainly, from the impoverished, "horse-riding" Indians.

Although Chickasaw planters did a brisk business in cotton and produce at Fort Washita, they were also exposed to repeated theft and assaults, as demonstrated by the complaints that members of the Love family leveled against the western Indians. Colonel Sloan Love, a Chickasaw district chief who owned forty-five slaves in 1847, had five horses stolen in one raid. The Keechi (a tribe from Texas) raiders also shot arrows at one of his slaves, who was injured.[51] In another raid, the exact date of which is unknown, a party of Comanches raided the Bob Love home and "killed all the slaves except one. This one crawled to the house full of arrows."[52] Several years later, Congress appropriated more than $7,000 in compensation to Overton Love for damages resulting from

Kiowa and Comanche raids (money drawn from those Indians' national funds).[53] Although the U.S. government permitted the Chickasaws "to go into Comanche country and look for their horses," they rarely recovered any of them because the Comanches sold the Chickasaws' stolen horses in Texas.[54] In 1851 Choctaw Robert Nail threatened vigilante action against Comanche raiders: "If we cannot receive any protection from these forts in our country, why then we must awake from our morbid lethargy, and put on our armor, and go to defend our rights and our country."[55] The U.S. government responded to Nail's threat of retaliation with a new fort.

Fort Arbuckle, constructed in 1851–52 a few miles west of Fort Washita as a complement to it, represented the high point of the federal government's efforts to secure peace on the Indian Territory–Texas frontier. In 1853 there were more than three thousand soldiers on the Texas frontier—the largest troop concentration in any single region since the war of 1812. The strength of this force played a large role in the decreased frontier violence of that year. Then the U.S. troops disappeared. More than one-third of the army forces were redeployed in response to the "Bleeding Kansas" crisis in 1855 and the Mormon War in 1857. The Chickasaws had to defend their own property against western Indians and a newly constituted group of Texas Rangers.[56]

In 1858 Major Douglas Cooper called the Chickasaws to arms and got an enthusiastic response. Major Cooper called on volunteers to "turn out for the defense of the frontier" and hunt down Comanche raiders. Over seventy men, mostly Chickasaws and a few Choctaws, answered Cooper's call. Cooper argued that the best way to end the Comanches' raids was to prove that the Chickasaws were still warriors. At this time, the presence of railroad surveyors angered the Comanches and prompted them to launch more frequent attacks on Chickasaw homesteads in the vicinity of Fort Arbuckle. The Chickasaws rightly feared the Comanches' retaliation for selling lands to whites. The *Daily National Intelligencer* reported the state of panic that elicited Cooper's unauthorized military response: "Large parties of Comanches were depredating nightly within a mile of this fort, and . . . as the country, was entirely destitute of troops, and the Indians a 'heap mad' very much apprehension existed lest they should make a descent upon the fort and destroy it, with the large amount of supplies it contained."[57] Chickasaw settlers moved into the fort for protection. Although Cooper's Indian battalion did not find any Comanches, Cooper believed that this show of strength disabused the Comanches' "minds of the idea that the Chickasaws and Choctaws or 'Wood Indians' as they are called, are afraid to go out on the plains and convinced them that no depredations on the frontier will be allowed to pass unpunished."[58]

The Chickasaws' combined fear of the Comanches and the Texans contributed to their decision to ally with the Confederate states. By treaty, the United States had agreed to maintain garrisons to guard the Chickasaws "from marauding bands of whites and wild Indians." However, the U.S. government abandoned Fort Washita and Fort Arbuckle in 1861 to fight Indians on the Plains, leaving the Chickasaws and Choctaws completely at the mercy of the western tribes (and Texan intruders). Governor Cyrus Harris (great-grandson of Major William Colbert) of the Chickasaw Nation called for a meeting of the Five Tribes to consider an alliance with the Confederacy. He explained that the federal government had ignored his request to "supply him with arms to protect the nation."[59] Chickasaw Sippia Paul, the daughter of Smith Paul, the founder of Pauls Valley, noted: "When the war broke out the Government removed the troops from Fort Arbuckle, taking away the protection for the Indians, so the Chickasaws were compelled through force of circumstances to enlist with the Confederates." She explained that "wild Indians from Texas and what is now Western Oklahoma . . . came into this section of the country killing and robbing people."[60]

In the Treaty of 1866, the U.S. government compelled the defeated Chickasaw Confederates to receive the Comanches, Witchitas, and other dislocated Indians into the western third of the country, the area known as the Leased District.[61] The Chickasaws had leased these lands to the federal government in 1855 (thus the name Leased District). By the Treaty of 1866, the Chickasaws and Choctaws allegedly forfeited their claim to continued ownership of these lands (that was the Supreme Court's decision). The Chickasaws never received more than a onetime rental payment. In the short term, the western reservations failed to improve the security of Chickasaw property because the U.S. government supplied the Comanches and other western Indians with inadequate provisions. The reservation Indians continued to live off the Choctaws' and Chickasaws' lands and property.[62] After the U.S. government cut their rations still further, Comanche warriors stepped up their raids on Chickasaw farms and ranches. A Comanche war party killed former district chief Edmund Pickens's son David with a poison arrow.[63]

The beleaguered Chickasaws borrowed stereotyped images of the Comanches and other displaced Indian groups from Americans. Governor Cyrus Harris requested authority to raise a troop of militia in 1868, explaining: "In order to save life and property, we have got to shoulder our arms and march." Harris, a wealthy planter of mixed descent, articulated a frontier view of the Comanches that might have come from a Texan. He reported that "no less than four thousand head of horses have been taken out of the country by these very naked fellows, who now live and foster on government provision, under the cloak of a treaty." He insisted that force alone would put down the "Mr. Wild Indian," and threatened to "call on the Choctaws for assistance to stop the ingress of all naked tribes into our nation." He warned that his next letter would "inform you of war."[64]

Gradually, relations between the western Indians in the Leased District and the citizens of the Chickasaw Nation improved. In part this was because the United States set up agencies in the Indian reservations carved out of the Leased District. It was also because the western Indians began to raise revenue by leasing range to Chickasaw and other Five Tribes' ranchers. Now, instead of raiding homesteads in lean times, the western Indians rustled cattle from the herds (sometimes owned by Chickasaws) grazing on their lands.[65]

In the 1880s several Chickasaw ranchers were crowded out of the Chickasaw Nation by cattlemen from Texas (some married to Chickasaw women) to the lands leased by the Chickasaws and Choctaws to the U.S. government for the use of the western Indians. Chickasaw Montfort Johnson left the most detailed record of such experiences. In 1889 he moved six thousand cattle to the Witchitas and affiliated bands' reservation in the Leased District, contracting to pay 6¢ an acre for exclusive grazing rights in an agreement approved by a U.S. agent. Johnson's son Edward worried about the location of the range, which lay just across the river from the Cheyenne and Arapaho reservation. Sometimes Cheyenne warriors demanded heavy tributes from cattlemen for the privilege of driving herds through their country, and they occasionally destroyed fences, burned ranges, and plundered cattle herds.[66]

While Johnson had thousands of cattle, the Cheyenne and Arapaho Indians lacked bare necessities like food and clothing. On account of the Cheyennes' extreme poverty, cattle theft was "not considered a crime any longer, even if it is found out." U.S. Indian agents reported that friendly western chiefs, even those considered the most civilized of their people, now nodded with approval at raids on the outsiders' cattle. The Cheyennes knew that the authorities could no nothing to stop them. One official admitted that it was impossible to "make arrests for offenses committed in which so many are interested."[67]

In the winter of 1889, Cheyenne Indians began to slaughter Johnson's cattle, for his herds had crossed onto their reservation. Agent Charles Ashley notified Johnson that his cattle were trespassing and "had destroyed fields of corn belonging to the Indians." When Johnson took no action, the Cheyennes and Arapahos acted decisively. Agent Ashley reported that the Cheyennes had rounded up Johnson's cattle and demanded a tax of a dollar a head for their release, which Johnson refused to pay.[68]

Cheyenne chief Whirlwind maintained that his people were "hard up for beef and for rawhide to make their moccasins' soles and valises and trunks of," and witnesses reported that they made use of every inch of Johnson's slaughtered cattle. One of Johnson's sons "found numbers of heads and feet where [the Cheyenne Indians] had butchered them and just left the feet; and very often I would find places where they had just emptied out the offal of the entrails."[69] In the summer of 1890, Whirlwind led a delegation to the Fort Reno agency to complain again of Johnson's intruding cattle.

In the meantime, Johnson filed a claim against the U.S. government for his livestock that had disappeared on the Cheyenne and Arapaho reservation. He claimed the loss of twenty-five hundred cattle and over a hundred horses. Congress denied compensation to him on the grounds that his losses had not occurred from the Cheyennes' aggression on the Chickasaws' lands—rather, his losses had resulted from his cattle and horses trespassing on the Cheyennes' and Arapahos' lands. In

1900 the Supreme Court refuted Johnson's and the Chickasaw Nation's contention that they still owned the Leased District, which included the Cheyenne and Arapaho reservation.[70] Without their consent or adequate compensation, the Chickasaws had been forced to share some of their new homeland with western Indians.

In sum, the Chickasaws' fear of property losses and personal harm, as well as American society's stereotypes of Indian savagery, worked together to shape the Chickasaw government's increasingly intolerant stance toward the Comanches and other western Indians. Their desire for their own exclusive lands contributed to their increasingly rigid definition of Chickasaw identity. They were civilized, not "wild" Indians, a point they emphasized in the Treaty of 1866 by demanding that they be referred to as "nations" while the western Indians were called "tribes."[71]

To some extent, many Chickasaws' experience of property and personal loss turned them against the western Indians. But also, Chickasaw leaders articulated white prejudices as a strategy to safeguard their nation. Fearful that their association with warlike bands would result in the loss of their self-government and lands, the Chickasaws drew a sharp line between themselves and the western Indians. The Chickasaw Nation's privileged status helped to restrain Texas Rangers from trespassing on their lands and to safeguard their relative autonomy. Because whites perceived the Chickasaws as culturally, if not racially, different from the western Indians, the Chickasaws were not squeezed onto reservations with semidependent Indian peoples.

3
Decision Not to Adopt Former Slaves, 1866–1907

The Chickasaws' struggle for autonomy and tribal independence involved strained relations with the Choctaws, western Indians, and their former slaves. After the Civil War, the Chickasaws were confronted with the consequences of the abolition of slavery. There were about two thousand freedpeople scattered among seven thousand persons in the Chickasaw Nation.[1] In 1866 the Chickasaw government negotiated a joint treaty with the Choctaw and U.S. governments. Since many Chickasaws had fought on the side of the Confederacy, the nation accepted terms of surrender.

The Treaty of 1866 required that the Choctaw and Chickasaw Indians abolish slavery and cede the Leased District lands to the federal government. The treaty tied the payment for the Leased District cession ($300,000) to the emancipation of the Chickasaw and Choctaw slaves and their settlement on Indian lands. Later, the justices of the U.S. Court of Claims pointed out the unfairness of the Treaty of 1866, which involved "the taking by the white man, for a consideration to be applied to the benefit of the black man, some millions of acres of land belonging to the red man." The only way that the Chickasaws could obtain their portion of the $300,000 was by "surrendering its equivalent [in lands] to the blacks."[2] In the event that the Chickasaws and the Choctaws refused to adopt their former slaves, the federal government would then use these funds to relocate their freedpeople to lands set aside for the Plains Indians in the Leased District. (There was never any consideration of relocating their former slaves outside of Indian Territory.)

Unlike treaties the United States brokered with the other Five Tribes, that with the Chickasaws and Choctaws included a provision stating that if the nations refused to adopt their freedpeople in two years' time, the federal government would remove them. The Chickasaws declined their share of the Leased District funds, requesting that the U.S. government use the funds to remove the freedpeople from the Chickasaw Nation. Although the U.S. government failed to uphold its end of the bargain, the removal clause gave the Chickasaws and Choctaws judicial leverage. When U.S. policy makers criticized the Chickasaws and Choctaws for their failure to adopt freedpeople, tribal leaders pointed out that they demanded only what was guaranteed them by treaty— the removal of the freedpeople from their lands.[3]

With the exception of the Seminoles, the other Five Tribes had to be bullied into the adoption of their former slaves. The Seminoles, along with the Creeks and Cherokees, adopted their freedpeople almost immediately; the Choctaws did so reluctantly in the 1880s; and the Chickasaws refused entirely. Trouble between the Chickasaws and their freedpeople came about largely because the federal government attempted to impose its will and additional financial burdens on the Chickasaw Nation. The Chickasaws resisted the intrusion of U.S. authority into their domestic affairs. In response to the U.S. government's demands that the Chickasaws grant freedpeople lands and suffrage, the Chickasaw Nation—members of both Progressive and National political affiliations—mobilized against granting blacks citizenship in their nation.

Beginning in the late eighteenth century, some Chickasaws and other southeastern Indians emulated white slaveholders, adopting plantation agriculture and intermarrying with whites. Within all the southern Indian nations, except for the Seminole, slavery was viewed as a key component of white civilization.[4] U.S. agents, missionaries, and white planters encouraged the Chickasaws to emulate Americans, and one of the ways they did this was by becoming slaveholders. By this means, Indian men could become agriculturalists, traditionally defined as women's work, without forfeiting male pride. At the time of Indian Removal, 225 Chickasaws out of approximately 4,000 owned slaves. They had a higher percentage of slaves than any other of the Five Tribes (Cherokee slaves were 15 percent, Choctaw slaves were 14 percent, and Creek slaves were 10 percent of their respective populations).[5]

In the decades following their forced relocation to Indian Territory, some slaves experienced increased autonomy and mobility, with some even obtaining their freedom. Slavery was less essential to the Chickasaws' economy than was true of most other slave systems, for the Chickasaws had a large, free farming population and poor access to cotton markets. Only the mixed-blood communities settled in the vicinity of Fort Washita and Boggy Depot grew much cotton, which was a far more labor-intensive undertaking than growing cereal crops or raising cattle. As a freedman recalled, most slaves "did not raise much cotton, but we raised corn, grain, and vegetables," cared for livestock, and performed household chores.[6] Some slaves lived apart from their masters, to whom they paid a tax in corn. Masters granted these slaves comparative autonomy in order to reduce the cost of providing for them.[7]

Observers remarked that Charles Cohee, a slave owned (and probably fathered) by Chickasaw planter James Colbert, dressed and acted as an Indian, wearing his straight hair long in the manner of Chickasaw hunters. In 1837 Cohee migrated west with the Colbert family. He did not receive annuities earmarked for Chickasaw citizens, but it is likely that he gained his freedom, as he was classified in the immigrant muster roll as a "Negro" rather than a "slave." Like many other persons of mixed African-Indian descent, Cohee was bilingual; he spoke both English and Chickasaw. He was also probably well versed in the sign language that traders used to communicate with the Comanches. For these reasons, Cohee served as an official interpreter at Chickasaw national council meetings.[8]

In the 1850s Cohee appears again in Chickasaw records as a member of several failed trading expeditions to the Comanches and Osages. White merchant J. H. Humphreys, who headed a plundered trading party, appealed to the U.S. government for restitution of the stolen goods. From Humphreys's perspective, Cohee was simply a Chickasaw. Humphreys noted that he "Started from his residence . . . accompanied by . . . Charley Cohee (Chickasaw), Tushkutimbe (Chickasaw), Simon (Choctaw) and colored boy belonging to . . . HoThlyche (called Billy)." Unlike Billy, who was singled out as a Negro and a slave, Cohee was designated simply as "Chickasaw." This record suggests that traders and ordinary Chickasaws regarded Cohee as a fellow citizen.[9]

By the mid-nineteenth century, according to the Chickasaw census of 1847, one quarter of Chickasaw household heads owned one or more slaves. A few planters, largely of mixed white and Indian ancestry, owned most of the slaves, while the large majority of tribe members owned only a few or, in by far the most cases, none at all. Even under the Choctaw and Chickasaw governments' repressive slave codes, which were modeled after those of the southern states, Indian-black segregation was a policy goal, rather than a reflection of reality. The Works Project Administration (WPA) interviews with freedpeople suggest that *mustee,* or part-Indian, part-black children, were as common in Indian Territory as mulatto children were in the southern states, where they comprised 10 percent of the black population. According to these firsthand accounts, small farmers regarded their slaves differently from commercially oriented planters, who saw the blacks' identity as inferior and their position as permanent.[10]

Because planters tended to become more involved in politics and the process of lawmaking, their desire to enforce strict racial boundaries eventually prevailed. Planters generally had better educations than small farmers and were bilingual. Often their countrymen deferred to them in politics because of their greater ability to negotiate with U.S. policy makers and to understand complicated financial arrangements. While merchants and cattlemen conducted business with men like Cohee, Chickasaw planters objected to their anomalous presence in a hierarchical plantation society in which most blacks remained enslaved.[11] As they gained control of the Chickasaws' constitutional government, planters created an increasingly restrictive environment for blacks, slave or free. The Chickasaw constitution of 1856 excluded "negroes and their descendents" from adoption to citizenship and prohibited the Chickasaw government from emancipating slaves without compensation to owners.[12] With sectional tensions rising between the American North and South, Chickasaw planters feared the day when they would be forced to free their 975 slaves who, by this time, on the eve of the Civil War, comprised nearly 20 percent of the nation's population and a good portion of the planters' assets.[13]

Taking their cue from their white neighbors, in 1857 and 1858 the Chickasaw legislature passed additional laws whose primary aim was to bar blacks from citizenship. An act of 1857 prohibited "negroes and their descendents" from voting or holding office in the nation. In 1858 the Chickasaw legislature denied blacks civil rights, stating that "no negro or descendant of a negro shall have any of the rights, privileges, and immunities of citizens of this nation." Judges were to discount the testimony of blacks in court against any but another "Negro." Another act passed that year outlawed the cohabitation of Indians and "Negroes" on pain of a heavy fine or jail term.[14] Following the lead of the white communities of neighboring Texas, the Chickasaw government drew a wider legal distinction between Indians and black slaves.

Under the Chickasaw legal system, children of black slave women (even if they had Chickasaw fathers) followed their mothers into slavery. This custom may not have reflected Chickasaw traditional matrilineality so much as a different standard imposed to aid the planter class. As scholars of slavery have long recognized, matrilineality in a slave society helped to perpetuate slavery since masters' having children by slave women produced more slaves.

The Chickasaw custom of matrilineality, however, dictated that Chickasaw women's children be recognized as tribal members. The offspring resulting from the union of a Chickasaw woman and a black man were adopted into the tribe. Such children were rare, because social ostracism discouraged most Chickasaw women from having sexual liaisons with black men. Nonetheless, it was possible for a few children of mixed African and Chickasaw ancestry to be absorbed into the Chickasaw Nation. A small minority of blacks in the nation had Chickasaw relatives who acknowledged and protected them.[15] Perhaps this explains why, in the aftermath of the Civil War, Chickasaw governor Winchester Colbert, himself a former slaveholder, found "great diversity of opinion among the people as to the status of the negro among us."[16]

In the U.S. government's view, the best way to solve the "Negro question" in Indian Territory was to reclassify the Chickasaws' former slaves as Indians. The Chickasaw and Choctaw delegates to the Treaty of 1866 objected to this policy. They saw the provisions of the 1866 treaty as just another way for the U.S. government to strip away their vested property in slaves and lands. Governor Colbert exhorted slaveholders not to free their slaves until Chickasaw delegates learned "whether or not they could get pay for them," and if not, they should drive them south to Texas.[17] Ultimately, Governor Colbert was responsible for drafting and executing the Chickasaw Nation freedpeople's emancipation document on October 11, 1866.

As did legislatures in the surrounding states, in the Reconstruction period the Chickasaws and Choctaws passed Black Codes, which restricted freedpeople's mobility and relegated them to second-class status. Still, white reporters maintained that "the freedmen are better treated in the Territory than in the United States."[18] Freedpeople's postwar circumstances varied in significant ways. In 1861 Nero Perry's Chickasaw master James McLish died, and Perry moved into his cabin on Caddo Creek. He lived alone there untroubled for decades, hunting for subsistence.[19] Generally, Chickasaw freedpeople gathered together in separate all-black or nearly all-black communities for mutual aid. One newspaper noted in 1877 that three thousand Chickasaw freedpeople "live to themselves and . . . are allowed to live upon and cultivate farms."[20] Most Chickasaws took little notice of them until freedpeople demanded absolute title to sections of land.

The Freedmen's Petition of 1869 excited the Chickasaws' worst fears, for in it freedpeople requested that Congress "sectionalize" Chickasaw lands. They further stated that they favored "opening this Territory to White Immigration and of selling to them, for the benefit of the whole people of these nations, our surplus lands."[21] To garner support from Americans, they wholly supported congressional plans to partition the Chickasaws' tribal domain and open the Indian Territory to white settlers.[22]

Encouraged by citizenship lawyers, freedpeople directed their energies toward winning Chickasaw and Choctaw citizenship. In 1870, at a joint Chickasaw-Choctaw freedpeople convention in Scullyville in the Choctaw Nation, the delegates demanded full integration into the Indian nations with an equal share of the Indians' tribal lands and annuities and full participation in their government and schools.[23]

While the Choctaws stalled in their decision about what to do about the freedpeople, the Chickasaws, under the leadership of Governor Benjamin F. Overton, were decisive in demanding their expulsion after 1874. Overton stated that Choctaw governor Coleman Cole was deluding himself if he believed that he could let the freedpeople remain in the nation without any privileges of citizenship. Overton warned the Chickasaw legislature not to adopt the freedpeople: "If you do, you sign the death warrant of your Nationality with your own hands; for the negroes will be the wedge with which our country will be rent asunder and opened up to the whites."[24] After Overton's speech, the Chickasaw legislature adopted a resolution providing for a joint tribal commission to agree upon "some plan for removing and keeping the freed people from the Choctaw and Chickasaw Country."[25]

In 1887 Congress passed the General Allotment Act, also known as the Dawes Act after its sponsor, U.S. senator Henry L. Dawes of Massachusetts. The act forced the Indians to relinquish their common land title and accept allotment, or individualized partitions of their lands. Federal policy focused specifically on breaking up reservations and tribal governments. The land grab was justified as a way to assimilate Indians faster by making them responsible for their own farms. While the Allotment Act exempted the Five Tribes, the Chickasaws saw that it was only a matter of time before Congress extended the law to them (1893). They became resentful of freedpeople's efforts to gain tribal land at the expense of all that they held dear—their common land system and tribal government.

Many Chickasaws believed that if enfranchised, freedpeople would compromise tribal resistance to the Allotment Act. They would use their voice in tribal affairs to fracture the tribal domain because they wanted their own homesteads. In a memorial to Congress, the Chickasaw government charged that "if invested with the elective franchise, [freedpeople] will be able to take possession of the government, and ultimately to deprive the Chickasaw people of their government and country."[26]

As the population of freedpeople grew, so the Chickasaws' hostility toward them intensified. The Chickasaws pointed out that the freedpeople's "natural increase has been much greater than that of the Indian" and that they had been joined by former slaves from the States. In 1888 Chickasaw leaders tried to impress U.S. officials with figures: "In two of the four counties of the Chickasaw nation, viz., Pickens and Pontotoc, the negroes outnumber the Indians, and in the third county, they would constitute half of the voting population."[27] The freedpeople countered that the Chickasaws exaggerated the numbers. Purportedly, the Chickasaws failed to mention Panola County because Chickasaw planters had driven freedpeople out of that region.[28] But in the 1880s the demographic trend was unmistakable. As a result of rumors that blacks would be able to obtain cheap land in Indian Territory, the number of blacks there grew. Blacks fleeing Texas swelled the black population of the Chickasaw Nation by several thousand. By 1890 the number of free blacks surpassed that of Indians in the Chickasaw Nation.[29]

The most important issue that mobilized the Chickasaw government against the freedpeople was the blacks' potential political power. Chickasaw leaders warned of a day in the not-so-distant future when their former slaves would seize control of tribal affairs and institutions: "The number of freedmen being so great, if adopted, will soon control our schools and government that we have been building and fostering for the past forty years. We love our homes, institutions, and government, and will not surrender them."[30] Some tribal members argued that blacks were unfit for citizenship and full political participation. As one Chickasaw warned, "If negroes were made citizens they would take charge of the Government and convert it into Hayti."[31]

Chickasaw leaders of both political parties favored the relocation of freedpeople to Oklahoma Territory in lieu of their adoption as Chickasaw citizens. Sam Paul, a Chickasaw politician of the Progressive Party, favored allotment, yet he disapproved of the U.S. government's attempt to force the Chickasaws to adopt their former slaves. On his return from Washington, D.C., as a Chickasaw delegate, Paul told reporters, "It is generally conceded at Washington that Oklahoma will be designed for the negro, in which case now is the time for the Chickasaw freedmen to secure to themselves a home and a country of their own." Paul spoke at an assembly of freedpeople to explain to them the advantages of relocation. He was an active proponent of resettling the freedpeople in Oklahoma Territory and offered to assist their exodus.[32]

The Chickasaw freedpeople formed a separate lobbying group, the Freedmen's National Rights Association, with Charles Cohee at its head. Cohee led the Chickasaw freedpeople's struggle for education, lands, and suffrage. He represented the black community of Berwyn, composed of about three hundred free blacks, in negotiations with U.S. officials, and he reported on general living conditions there. In Cohee's view, freedpeople were "deprived of some privileges that a free people o[ugh]t to have." As president of the Chickasaw Freedmen's Association, Cohee urged the U.S. government to intervene before "another generation must bear through life the blight of wrong and injustice which were inflicted upon their mothers and fathers." He pointed out that in all the other Five Tribe nations, blacks enjoyed greater privileges and material benefits than the Chickasaw freedpeople.[33]

In demanding Chickasaw citizenship, some freedpeople emphasized their Indian blood. The Chickasaws claimed that the degree of purity of their blood was as high "as in any other southern community." That may have been the case; nevertheless, a special census taken by the United States in 1890 identified 122 "Negro Chickasaws" and 9 "Mulatto Chickasaws" in the category of Chickasaws. This list included only biracial individuals who had Chickasaw mothers. The numbers of "Negro Chickasaws" would have been much higher (up to 1,000) if Chickasaw individuals with black mothers and Indian fathers had been counted.[34]

Freedwomen among the Five Tribes may have had numerous progeny outside of wedlock because Indian men were discouraged from marrying the black mothers of their children.[35] The Chickasaw Freedmen Association's lawyer identified "a number of the Negroes of said Nation who possess from one-half to two thirds and even three fourths of Indian blood."[36] They remained legally invisible, however, because they were illegitimate. In 1906 one senator who investigated freedpeople's claims remarked that "instances in which we found that the Indians were lawfully or legally married to negroes were so scarce that I have no recollection of one now. It is almost impossible, in enrollment matters of the various nations, for people of mixed blood, African and negro blood, to show a lawful or legal marriage between the parties."[37]

In seeking recognition as Chickasaw freedpeople, many blacks confronted their ambiguous origins. Freedwoman Emma Thompson Hampton stated that her mother, a slave in the Chickasaw Nation, "looked like a full blood Indian" but was recognized as "a negress." She did not know who her father was.[38] In 1907 two thousand persons claimed to have Chickasaw blood, sometimes on their father's side, but the Chickasaws rejected all claims that were based on descent from an Indian father and black mother, the tribal status of the child always taking that of the mother.[39]

Cohee protested that freedpeople were never given an opportunity to prove their Indian blood and add their names to the Chickasaws' annuity rolls. The Chickasaws insisted that their claims were invalid, since they were based on patrilineal descent.[40] Governor Douglas Johnston explained: "There are, in the Choctaw and Chickasaw nations, from 1,000 to 2,000 persons, the descendants of freedmen or negro mothers, who claim to be the illegitimate descendants of Choctaw or Chickasaw fathers. . . . It was contended that these people . . . were possessed of some degree of Indian blood, and that they should be permitted to take and enjoy the status of their alleged fathers, without reference to recognition, tribal status, legitimacy or enrollment." This was, Johnston insisted, a new definition of tribal citizenship conjured up by enterprising citizenship lawyers.[41]

Freedman Thomas Randolph identified himself as "native" of the Chickasaw Nation, and therefore privileged by rights unavailable to blacks and others born outside of it. He explained to the secretary of the interior, "No one has ever intimated that I, being a native, had no right to all the land I could use not in use by any other native." Randolph continued, "I only wish to have what I am entitled to as a native, being the fact that I am a colored man."[42] Blacks from the States were not entitled to Indian lands, thus Randolph's emphasis that he and his wife were born in Indian Territory. Randolph demanded the rights due him as a freedman, having heard that in other Indian nations freedpeople fared much better. He inquired of the secretary of the interior, "What and how much right have we the collard [sic] citizens of the five civilized tribes in said nations of the Indian Territory." Randolph supposed that the 1866 treaty agreement between the United States and the Chickasaws permitted native blacks to farm forty acres. Randolph had the misfortune of situating his farm and family on a railroad hub that a powerful real estate company desired and was violently dispossessed of his homestead, farm, and possessions.[43]

Freedpeople like Randolph asserted a broader right to Chickasaw citizenship based on their cultural identification with the Indians. As one historian nicely summarized it, freedpeople argued that their shared history "should prevail in identifying individuals and determining their attendant legal status and rights."[44] In addition to their shared experience of Indian Removal, freedpeople stated that they were identified by custom with the Chickasaws. Generations of slave families had lived among the Chickasaws, adopting their diet, language, medicine, and dress and speaking "the languages as fluently as the natives themselves."[45] The argument of cultural affinity left an impression upon U.S. politicians of the Republican Party, who were predisposed to resolve the freedpeople question in the freedpeople's favor, but failed to sway the Chickasaws, who jealously guarded their autonomy and tribal inheritance.

Beleaguered Chickasaw politicians placed increasing emphasis on ethnic consciousness as a fundamental element of Chickasaw nationalism. From 1876 Governor Overton had warned his people that freedpeople were dangerous to the Chickasaws' ethnic integrity. Decades later, Governor Johnston placed greater emphasis on the Chickasaws' racial composition, for he understood Americans' obsession with racial categorization; a drop of African blood made a person black. Governor Johnston expressed his people's fears of being labeled a "Negro" nation. He noted that whites expressed "no feeling of prejudice against my people. They are received upon an equal footing with all other citizens of our State." Johnston suspected that the U.S. government would use the declining Indian blood quantum as a rationale for stripping the Chickasaws of entitlements derived from their Indian status, such as lands, annuities, and other treaty guarantees. Johnston posed a rhetorical question: "Will this continue if our citizenship is debased by the addition of many of our former slaves and their descendants? Will not discrimination and prejudice take the place of equality and fraternity?"[46] The Chickasaws did not have to look far to see discrimination. In the new State of Oklahoma, blacks were relegated to separate schools and bathrooms.[47] Johnston maintained that legislation forcing the Chickasaw Nation to adopt blacks threatened to rob them of their racial pride, "which our people have so long cherished." He stated that white officials could take the Chickasaws' lands and money, just as long as they "keep our rolls pure."[48]

The Chickasaws stood to lose their special status as Indians and be categorized as "coloreds" if they incorporated over four thousand freed-people into their nation.[49] This led them not only to resist adopting their freedpeople but also to protest their inclusion in the Chickasaw allotment rolls. In order to receive their land allotment, the Chickasaws had to enroll with the Bureau of Indian Affairs (BIA). Each individual's name then went on the "Dawes rolls," through which the BIA determined eligibility for land distribution. Many court cases resulted, as the Chickasaws contested hundreds of persons, mostly whites, who fraudulently enrolled as citizens in order to receive lands and annuities.

The Dawes Commission established separate freedpeople rolls. The segregated rolls solidified racial lines among Indians and free blacks, even among the Seminoles, who had not strictly maintained them. The Chickasaw government's resolve against incorporating freedpeople into the nation meant that freedpeople with Chickasaw blood derived little, if any, benefits from their bloodlines. For example, in 1898 freedman Charles Cohee Jr. enrolled to receive part of the Chickasaws' lands as a Chickasaw freedman. Although Cohee was entitled to Chickasaw citizenship (under rules drawn up by the Dawes Commission) based on his Chickasaw heritage (his father was a Chickasaw), and thus to a greater portion of lands, he elected instead to stake a smaller and surer claim to forty acres on the freedpeople's rolls, which encompassed a broader category, including all former slaves, regardless of whether or not they had Indian heritage. Cohee (he and his wife had six children to support) and others were intimidated by U.S. enrollment administrators, who pressured them to enroll as freedpeople, rather than as Chickasaw citizens by blood. Cohee and many other freedpeople had farmed more extensive tracts than forty acres, and thus had to forfeit some of the property they had cultivated. Enrollment agent Tams Bixby allegedly promised to transfer Cohee's name to the tribal rolls at a later date but failed to do so.

In the early 1900s some five hundred Chickasaw freedpeople received land allotments of forty acres. In 1902 Cohee tried unsuccessfully to get his name transferred from the freedpeople rolls to the Chickasaw rolls in order to acquire another hundred acres. Frustrated by his failure, Cohee argued that he and other blacks who had "Chickasaw blood in our veins" had a right to be listed near their blood relatives on the Chickasaw rolls. He asked U.S. officials to empower black Chickasaws to present evidence of their Chickasaw ancestry with the end goal of transferring them to the Chickasaw Indian roll of citizens. He noted that he took pride in his Indian heritage but received few tangible material or social benefits from this connection. Cohee and Randolph found themselves just slightly better off than ex-slaves in the States. While the Allotment Act doomed the Chickasaws as a tribal entity, it provided their former slaves with a stake in Chickasaw lands. Eligible freedpeople received their own forty-acre allotments, although their children born after 1899 were not entitled to enroll and receive allotments, as Chickasaw children were.[50]

In the Supplemental Agreement to the General Allotment Act (1902), the Chickasaws secured a provision that the U.S. Court of Claims would decide whether the Chickasaw freedpeople, who were never adopted, had a right to allotment.[51] In 1904 the Chickasaws won a claims case in the Supreme Court, which granted them compensation for lands that the U.S. government distributed to freedpeople.[52] In 1910 the Chickasaws and Choctaws received $606,936.08 for the lands allotted to five hundred Chickasaw freedpeople (the lands were jointly owned by both tribes), and this money was appropriated and paid out per capita. The Chickasaws were not compensated for lands allotted to Choctaw freedpeople, however. They later sought remuneration for their interest in these lands, but failed in this suit because the Choctaws had adopted their freedpeople.[53]

Despite pressure from Congress and the Choctaws, the Chickasaws resisted freedpeople's campaigns for adoption for forty years. The Chickasaws maintained that it was their prerogative to determine eligibility for Indian citizenship and any abrogation of that right would undermine their sovereignty. They even went further, ending their former practice of limited racial inclusivity—that is, recognizing the citizenship of black children born of Chickasaw mothers—in order to avoid being cast as nonwhites in a segregationist society. In the process of transforming Indian Territory into part of Oklahoma, the U.S. government imposed a standard of race identification upon the peoples of the territory. Race became the identifier that determined which allotments could be sold, which allottees were competent and which were not, and which persons would become full citizens of the state.

The Chickasaws were successful in convincing Oklahomans that in a biracial society, they should be regarded as whites and admitted to white schools. An American newspaper presented the favored version of Chickasaw history: "None of their white neighbors have had more pride of race than they, and it has been their boast that Chickasaw blood is pure blood."[54] In 1907 the State of Oklahoma passed Jim Crow legislation that recognized Chickasaw and other "pure-blooded" Indians as white and everyone with African ancestry as black.

In the end, the Chickasaw government insisted that Indian ethnicity and not cultural attributes defined citizenship. To safeguard their tribal inheritance, the Chickasaws dismissed the claims of former slaves who grew up in the same surroundings and shared in their culture, treating freedpeople as a foreign people who had been and always would be strangers in Indian Territory. Thus, the Chickasaws advanced their social status in the new state of Oklahoma and kept more, but not much more, property in Chickasaw hands.

4
Right to Tax and Eject
U.S. Citizens, 1870s–1890s

In the late nineteenth century, a significant issue arose for the Chickasaws over their control of tribal lands and maintenance of political autonomy. Like the other members of the Five Tribes, the Chickasaws' sovereignty was undermined by the steady increase in the numbers of whites moving into the territory. If the cattle boom attracted free blacks and white suitors to the Chickasaw Nation in the 1870s, the prospect of cheap farm and grasslands attracted an even more dangerous group of noncitizens, namely, settlers.

With plentiful lands and an annual annuity, the Chickasaws had no need to farm for anybody else, and agricultural laborers were hard to come by. The labor shortage led some Chickasaw citizens to invite white laborers into the nation. By the laws of the Chickasaw Nation, any citizen was allowed to occupy any of the unoccupied lands in the nation. Citizens "could open a farm in any part of the public domain, provided that it did not encroach upon the property of another citizen."[1] It was not long before the "white" intermarried Indians and others occupied the most valuable lands and subleased them to other whites. These leasing arrangements devolved into a perversion of the Chickasaws' communal land system, wherein individual members hired dozens of white tenants or sharecroppers and established claims to large tracts of communal lands. Thus individual tribal members had caused a problem that the tribal government sought to remedy.

The Chickasaw government attempted to address the problem through taxation. To reclaim Chickasaw sovereignty and to drive out white intruders, the legislature passed permit laws that taxed noncitizens. Faced with an outcry from whites and Chickasaws adversely affected by the restrictive law, the Chickasaw government defended its legal right to levy fees upon noncitizens and to remove and exclude nonmembers.[2]

While some Chickasaws managed to turn a profit from leasing, the system undermined the tribe's continued existence as a political community. In addition to attracting an influx of foreigners, it created a deep political rift at a time when unity was needed to defeat federal challenges to tribal existence. As was the case in each of the Five Tribes, internal economic questions divided Chickasaw subsistence farmers from the commercial class.[3] Chickasaw George Nail explained it this way: "White immigration meant that tribal government had to give way, [it] split the nation into two parties—opening up the country and white men's ways versus the other side wanted this country for the Indians; they wanted Indian government, Indian ways, the land held in common by the tribe as a whole."[4]

Members of the Chickasaw Progressive Party defended their right to make money from leasing lands to whites. They argued that tribal prosperity followed from private gain. Progressives drew support from large-scale farmers who had white tenants, and from investors in railroad and mining corporations that wanted to gain a foothold in the nation.[5] Dr. Worthington, an intermarried white, urged his Chickasaw neighbors "to lease out their land, telling them that the game would soon be gone and that if they would rent out their land the rent would make them a living." His Chickasaw neighbors reportedly "scoffed at the idea" because they objected to the flood of whites entering their territory.[6] Another man stated that he objected to the lease system because he did not want "another white community among their [the Chickasaws'] own people." He and like-minded citizens had withdrawn "from the portion of the country which was occupied by white men."[7]

Small farmers' antagonism to the agricultural leasing system was shared by Chickasaw ranchers, who felt the pinch of dwindling range as whites moved into the territory and fenced the open ranges in their nation.[8] The National Party (also called the Pull-back Party) platform was to maintain the Chickasaws' communal land system and limit whites' access to these lands. The members of this party were not swayed by arguments that the tribal economy would develop more slowly without white laborers and corporations. They had no desire for wealth, and they wanted to safeguard their way of life. Long after Oklahoma achieved statehood, many Chickasaw farmers withdrew to isolated, relatively poor rural areas "where they tried to live as traditionally as possible."[9]

S. W. Marston, a Union agent (the Union was a U.S. agency created to oversee the Chickasaws and Choctaws), maintained that National candidate Governor Benjamin Overton (1874–78, 1880–84) "was elected chief or governor by the full-blood element of the nation under the pledge that he would have every white man removed out of the nation."[10] The son of white lumberman John Overton and mixed-blood Chickasaw Tennessee Allen, Overton was orphaned at a young age and reared by his Chickasaw uncles Isaac and Robert Love. He became a successful rancher. As governor, Overton lambasted Chickasaw entrepreneurs who exploited economic opportunities that he considered detrimental to the nation: "[White tenants] are the coadjutors and supporters of that class of [Chickasaw] citizens who are and have ever been persisting in their unlawful and treasonable course in attempting to break up the tribal rights of our people and open your country to settlement by foreign emigration, actuated by selfish motives only, and to foster which they would gladly welcome the downfall of their government and the ruin of their people."[11]

Overton stressed that his people needed to put their nation's interests before profits. He urged "every man of business" to "offer fair inducements for the labor of his own people" and to "dispense with foreign labor as rapidly as possible." While conceding that self-sufficiency would take time, Overton maintained that the Chickasaws had enough annuities to support them without relying on noncitizens for their sustenance.[12]

Under the liberal leasing system that Overton deplored, white tenants occupied Chickasaw lands free of charge with the understanding that when their lease expired, their improvements would revert to their Chickasaw landlord. One renter described his contract as a "running lease" requiring that during each year of the lease a certain number of acres be added to those already in cultivation. During this time, the tenant could keep the proceeds from all that he extracted from the land. After the lease expired, the tenant would have to move elsewhere or negotiate a new lease. This system enabled Chickasaws by marriage and by blood to increase the value of their lands without any cash investment. Freedwoman Rose Mercer and her husband leased eighty acres of land from a Chickasaw. She recalled, "The only thing asked was that it be improved." Another renter described his lease as "ground that had been given to some Indian's children and he wanted improvements on it without doing any work himself." The running lease system (theoretically) made farms "for Indian children by the time they reach maturity."[13] Many cases resulted in illegal financial "settlements" rather than the land and its improvements passing to Indian children.

White renters tried to make it seem as though they served the Chickasaws when in fact they held the Indians' land without adequate compensation. Zack Redford recalled the situation candidly when interviewed by the Federal Writers' Project in 1935. He said the leasing system amounted to "the Indian giving the white man a farm for twenty-four years. You could have as many acres as you could put into cultivation."[14]

Of course, opponents of the lease system charged that it endangered their children's prospects, for it permitted noncitizens to despoil the lands of their timber, minerals, and grass, leaving wasteland for future generations. Governor Overton explained that Chickasaws should reserve the benefits of their land for posterity: "We owe it to them that such of our domain as is not required for our own use should be kept for them, fresh and not despoiled of its timber."[15] Overton's concern was warranted. By the 1930s, the Chickasaws' agricultural lands were largely ruined by erosion on account of widespread deforestation, intensive agriculture, and cattle ranging.[16]

Before Overton took office as governor, the Chickasaw legislature had prohibited the leasing of lands to noncitizens for more than a year, but the law proved "a perfect failure" because it was not enforced. In defiance of the law, Chickasaw citizens by blood and intermarriage continued to grant leases for five, ten, and sometimes an indefinite number of years "for a mere trifle." Overton protested that under the arrangement, many noncitizens enjoyed economic benefits "equaling our own privileges which we alone should enjoy."[17] Although those non-Indians given authorization to fence off and use portions of tribal lands could not obtain title to the soil, "their enclosures were property in which they had almost all the rights that U.S. landholders enjoyed. They could buy, sell, subdivide, inherit, and lease out farms, ranches, and town lots, until vacant land became an endangered entity."[18]

The fencing practices of whites angered many Chickasaws, especially farmers who had moderate landholdings. They objected when whites "claimed and fenced off any section or part section of land and claimed it on their own."[19] Some whites reported meeting Indians who "won't let you stick a post in the ground . . . the Indians think that if there is a fence these parties would be more likely to take their land from them."[20] Chickasaw rancher Tubbee Cutch "was very prejudiced against the whites for coming in and fencing up the Indians land." He burned down the home of a white squatter because he "began fencing up some land and the Indians were not in favor of this."[21]

In the main, intermarried whites were most likely to abuse the lease system. First they engrossed thousands of acres of prime farmland, rangeland, coal land, and timberland, and then they subrented it to white noncitizens and agents of corporations. Many intermarried whites purposely set out to develop as much of the Chickasaw lands as they could, staking off thousands of acres for themselves and dozens of white friends and relatives. Irishman Frank Murray, the founder of Erin Springs, was one of the largest landholders in the nation. After Murray married Chickasaw Alzira McCaughey, he established an eight-thousand-acre farm and fenced in thousands of acres of pasture for his ten thousand head of cattle.[22]

Entire communities of white noncitizens coalesced around the farms of intermarried citizens. A virtual white township, the community of Randolph developed around intermarried citizen William C. Randolph's farm. Randolph's niece recounted, "My uncle . . . married a Chickasaw girl . . . which gave him a right to all the land he wanted to fence." A wagon train of whites immediately headed for Randolph's, where they built houses and corrals. His niece recalled, "All had to pay rent to my uncle."[23]

In the mid-1870s Smith Paul, father of Progressive Party leader Sam Paul, married a Chickasaw woman and invited dozens of white men and their families, some of them Indian and some of them not, to settle in what became known as Pauls Valley. The Paul family settled these immigrants on long-term leases and prospered when their settlement became a stagecoach depot on the line running between Caddo and Fort Sill.[24] Other white communities of friends and relatives sprouted on lands claimed by intermarried citizens Jack Lawrance and Sweet Price, to name a few.[25] Of the excessive enclosures controlled by "white" Chickasaw citizens and their relatives by marriage, one land-hungry congressman exaggerated for effect: "A score of Chickasaw citizens in whom combined there is hardly enough aboriginal blood to make a full-blood Indian, control nearly ninety percent of the arable lands of that nation."[26]

But even some Chickasaws by blood caught the speculative fever and engrossed large acres of land. For example, Chickasaw senator Nelson Chigley had two thousand acres of land under cultivation. His son reflected on his life: "He came to the Washita Valley in 1854 and began farming. He broke his land with oxen and homemade plows. Father was very industrious. He tried to teach others of his tribe who were not so ambitious to be economical and thrifty by living such a life himself."[27] A few decades later, Chigley hired fifty-three noncitizen laborers at one time to develop and expand his holdings.

Many Chickasaws by blood took advantage of the leasing system to a lesser degree than Chigley. Consider the case of Jane Brown, described as a full-blood Chickasaw widow who leased two hundred acres for ten years to a Texan. "He was to pay no rent but improve the place instead and . . . every year he hauled Mrs. Brown two loads of corn."[28] The arrangement was an amicable one, even though the Texan violated Chickasaw law by grazing a large herd of cattle on his leased lands.

Once white tenants entered Indian Territory, they commonly shirked their obligations to the Chickasaw government, if not to their landlord, and invited more friends and family members to join them on the Chickasaws' lands.[29] Getting the whites to move off the improved lands was a challenge. They were "seldom known to leave" and some refused to turn over the improved land to their Indian landlords. More than a few whites argued that since they had developed the land, they ought to own it. (They demanded outright ownership of their leases when the U.S. government began to subdivide and apportion the Chickasaws lands at the beginning of the twentieth century.)[30]

To discourage the use of white labor, Governor Overton tried to make it prohibitively expensive. When Overton took office, the annual permit law mandated a 25¢ occupancy tax for noncitizens. Overton urged a dramatic increase of the permit fee levied on white labor to enlarge the treasury and slow the erosion of Chickasaw lands.[31] In 1876, at Overton's recommendation, the legislature raised the fee to $5, and then in 1877 to $25 a year. The Chickasaw landholder was responsible for registering all his noncitizen labor and then collecting the permit fees from them, payable to the Chickasaw government. Chickasaw citizens who continued to employ noncitizens but refused to pay the permit fee would be fined.[32] The intent was to wipe out wealthy Indians' efforts to "lay claim to large tracts of valuable land and mineral resources in the public domain by employing white citizens . . . or by promising to divide that land with them once the Indian country became a territory of the United States."[33]

The permit law divided the Chickasaw electorate and triggered a violent outcry from whites and their Chickasaw allies. Chickasaws who relied upon white labor saw the law as counterproductive, if not downright dangerous, to the continued sovereignty of the tribal government. Progressive legislators demanded a reduction of the fee, whereas the Nationals supported the new law. A handful of Chickasaw businessmen wrote letters to Washington demanding to know whether Overton, and by implication the Chickasaw government, had the authority to enforce the new permit law. Chickasaws Robert Love and Benjamin Franklin Colbert petitioned U.S. officials for relief from the permit tax. In their letters they challenged the Chickasaw Nation's sovereignty over U.S. citizens. To Overton, their memorials represented nothing short of treason. He charged that since 1872 Lemuel Reynolds and the petitioners had accepted expensive gifts—bribes—from railroad agents.[34] Similarly, Choctaw chief Coleman Cole denounced the Chickasaw complainants, stating that they "[r]epresent a turbulent minority of the tribe with sinister motives."[35]

The Chickasaw government sent delegates to Washington, D.C., every year to oppose measures that would significantly weaken or end tribal government. Intermarried whites sent their own delegates, such as Reynolds, who unwittingly joined territorial lobbyists in undermining tribal sovereignty. In defiance of the Chickasaw legislature (of which he was an elected member), Reynolds protested the new permit tax on behalf of "thousands of industrious farmers in my nation." Reynolds argued that the tax would result in thousands of acres given over to weeds. This was the stance taken by Progressive Party newspapers. A reporter for the *Star Vindicator* alleged that the $25 permit fee would "completely paralyze farming operations" and "bring the Chickasaw Nation to the point of starvation."[36] Reynolds asked the Department of the Interior to "afford them relief from the exorbitant tax on labor to which they are now subjected."[37]

As Reynolds pointed out, a provision of the Treaty of 1866 invited whites skilled in agriculture to live and labor in the Chickasaw Nation. Overton countered that the intent of the treaty stipulation was to allow a few specialists that the government might invite into the nation to teach its citizens agriculture, not ordinary field hands. He regretted that some Chickasaws had taken advantage of the treaty clause "to introduce large number of laborers for the purpose of opening extensive farms."[38] Overton denounced Reynolds and the other Chickasaw opponents of the permit law in the strongest terms, "as grand villains and malicious liars and traitors to their country, who ought not to breathe the breath of life."[39]

Although usually motivated by personal self-interest, the Chickasaw objectors to the permit law raised some legitimate points. By the 1880s, it may have been too late to disentangle the national economy from the white permit system. It was politically impossible to remove all the whites who were benefiting from it, and it was unlikely that "the United States would furnish the agent with the soldiers necessary to enforce the law."[40] After all, the United States had refused to expel whites from the Chickasaws' lands in Mississippi, and more recently had failed to remove the Chickasaws' former slaves. Under treaty stipulations, the U.S. government was obligated to protect the Five Tribes from intrusion; failing that, the security of the Indian governments was severely compromised.[41]

Chickasaw attempts to enforce the permit law without U.S. soldiers provoked a defiant response from whites. One group of whites formed a Citizens' Association, which passed the following resolution: "While acknowledging the Indian ownership of land in the Chickasaw nation, we deny their right to collect 1 cent of tax from anyone but citizens of their [so-called] government."[42] The members of the group drew an absurd parallel between the supposedly tyrannical Chickasaw tax, their lack of representation, and the British Stamp Act of 1765. A reporter for the *Star Vindicator* warned that Overton's excessive permit fee would provoke the federal government to intervene in tribal politics: "[The Chickasaws] had better meet the government half way and get a good bargain than keep up strife until the government interferes."[43] A white criminal named Meeks fired nine buckshots at Overton, but failed to wound the governor.[44] The organized resistance to paying the permit fee and the failed attack on his life validated Overton's comments about whites' arrogant disregard for Chickasaw customs and laws: "[Americans] bid defiance to our laws as soon as they arrive in our lands, or at least as soon as they learn" that Chickasaws had no jurisdiction over them.[45]

In answer to angry whites' and Chickasaws' petitions, the U.S. Indian agent declared the permit law invalid on the grounds that the Chickasaw government needed to confer with him before taxing U.S. citizens. Then he turned the matter over to the secretary of the interior, Charles Schurz, who likewise voided Overton's permit law, this time asserting that the Chickasaw government needed the U.S. president's permission to tax U.S. citizens. Their decisions had far-reaching consequences, for the Union Agency was charged with the specific duty of removing intruders from the Chickasaws' lands. As a result of these high-level officials' misconstruction of the Chickasaws' treaty guarantees, many whites believed that they were authorized to "enter the country without the consent of the Indian authorities" and to refuse to pay the yearly tax.[46]

Overton remained convinced that he had the right to tax whites and regulate their immigration into the Chickasaw Nation, and he demanded a rehearing in the matter of the Chickasaw permit law: "The license afforded to bad white men by your decision will be well nigh intolerable," for it "deprives us of the power of governing them while they live in our midst." He cited treaty after treaty wherein the U.S. government had empowered the Chickasaws to punish white trespassers "as they please." As to white tenants' rights, Overton wrote, "The persons in question are not obliged to enter the Chickasaw nation. They can remain without, and so avoid the necessity of obtaining the permits." He also addressed the objections of Chickasaw landlords, arguing that the Chickasaw government had no obligation "to admit persons who desire to be employed by individual Indians, or whom individual Indians desire to employ."[47]

Pending the result of his appeal, Overton proceeded to collect the tax without the assistance of the U.S. Indian Agency. Several large landholders criticized Overton for using money from the permit fee to form and pay the members of his Indian militia. As much to attract publicity as to enforce the permit law, Overton marched from farm to farm at the head of the Indian militia evicting tax evaders. Reynolds implored Secretary Schurz to intervene before the farmers took up arms in self-defense. According to Reynolds, they would be "left the alternative of allowing our farms to go to waste or of defending what we know to be our rights the best we can."[48]

In WPA interviews, settlers related how difficult it was for the Chickasaw government to collect the permit fee. One settler recalled that "so many of the Indians were using white labor that they would have to pay for, they protested the act and much bitterness resulted."[49] Many white intruders (those whites who refused to buy permits) left before Overton's Indian militia arrived, and then returned quickly thereafter. As one observer remembered, "As soon as the militia had departed the people whom they had driven out, turned around and drove back to the Territory and went back to their homes to live until the permit collector came again."[50] One permit collector reported: "The non-citizens laugh at the idea of being put out of the country as they say they will beat the officers back."[51]

A few Chickasaws by marriage defended their "right" to nonpermitted white labor with force. Among the pistol-wielding tax evaders were Robert Love and his large community of white renters, who successfully evaded the tax. Chickasaw Oscar Lawrance remembered that his father, an intermarried white, was "arrested and put in jail at Tishomingo regularly once a year . . . [because he] refused to pay permits for his renters." That continued until the Lawrance boys became men and obstructed the Indian police's efforts to apprehend their father.[52]

Dozens of white tenants appealed to Washington officials to stop Overton's militia. J. W. Rogers wrote Secretary Schurz: "Since your decision Gov. Overton boasts that he has compelled white men to pay the tax in spite of you; and he declares that if he is prevented from enforcing the tax from white men he will compel chickasaw citizens to pay $25 for every white person they employ to work on their farms."[53] Another white man wrote, "His Excellency Gov. B. F. Overton says he will collect the permit ($25) or sink the nation."[54]

The problem of white intruders was so great among all the Five Tribes that despite the outcry in the Chickasaw Nation, the Choctaw and Cherokee governments followed the Chickasaw example and also raised the permit fee in their nations to $25. Because Cherokee juries refused to convict the violators of the law, the legislation was soon repealed. In his "Message" of 1877, Overton asked the Chickasaw legislature to retain the permit law at $25 and the courts to enforce it because it was "a wall of safety and protection."[55]

In 1879 the U.S. Senate Judiciary Committee upheld the Five Tribes' right to tax U.S. citizens residing in their nations. Led by former Supreme Court justice David Davis, the committee concluded that the Chickasaws were "invested with the right of self-government and jurisdiction over the persons and property within the limits of the territory they occupy" and thus their government could "resort to taxation" to maintain peace and improve their condition. Moreover, the tax was warranted because the white intrusion was "injurious to the well-being of the Indians."[56] The U.S. attorney general Wayne MacVeagh seconded the decision, giving further validation to the Chickasaw and Choctaws' permit laws and their right to levy fees on noncitizens.[57]

Although the rulings favored the Chickasaws, they were not widely publicized in territorial newspapers, and those who knew of the Senate's decision just ignored it and continued to assert their right to farm Chickasaw lands without any payment to the Chickasaw government. In truth, the Chickasaw government failed to consistently enforce the permit law. After Overton left office in 1878 due to a constitutional term limit, the new Chickasaw governor, Benjamin Burney (1878–80), reduced the permit fee to $5 and welcomed whites and white corporations back into the nation.[58] Although Burney ran as a National Party candidate and won votes on the basis of his association with Overton, his brother-in-law, he made a variety of concessions to Overton's opponents.[59] The new governor said that Overton's $25 permit tax had engendered "anger and prejudice . . . between the white people and the Indians."[60] During Burney's two-year term, white intruders were allowed to pour into the nation. Certainly, his supporters felt betrayed.

In Burney's view, which was also the Progressive Party's position, high taxes discouraged the farming interests of the nation and retarded the Chickasaws' progress. Burney stated that on account of Overton's excessive permit fee, Chickasaw "farms lay idle and unproductive and much of the money paid to us by the United States had to be paid to the people as an annuity to keep them from want."[61] Burney himself had several white tenants and enjoyed a position of prestige as the leader of the small community of whites that grew up around his farm. The Reverend J. H. Dickerson recalled that Burney often visited his white tenants to "read, talk, and pray with them."[62] One of Burney's renters said of him: "While he stood by his own people, he liked the white man's way of living best."[63]

Returned to office in 1880, Overton charged that Burney's administration had "totally disregarded and virtually suspended" the laws he had pushed through for the greater good of the people and the survival of their national existence.[64] Overton regretted that "the spirit of the law was defeated, which all, friend and foe, will admit was broad and comprehensive enough to protect the entire people in their tribal form of government." He set out to reverse the damage done during his predecessor's tenure. Overton's animosity toward Burney's policies did not extend to the man: he appointed Burney superintendent of education and attributed his shortcomings as governor to his frequent illness during his administration, which had led to a "want of energy in executing and putting in full force the laws of the Nation."[65] But Burney betrayed Overton by serving as an advocate for Texas stockmen's demand for grazing contracts in Chickasaw lands.[66] In retaliation Overton fired the superintendent of education, alleging that Burney had neglected his duties.[67]

Overton now faced a greater challenge than he had during his first two administrations. Not only were large cattle companies invading the Chickasaws' range, white squatters were moving onto Chickasaw lands without any intention of following Chickasaw laws or paying for their right to be there. Federal indecision about the Indians' authority over U.S. residents living among the Five Tribes had encouraged the latest wave of intruders. As U.S. Indian agent John Q. Tufts observed, on account of the "undecided policy" toward white tenants, hundreds of whites built "farms and are living today in that country without permission from anybody."[68]

Again Overton gathered his Indian police, and with the help of U.S. soldiers attempted to dislodge thousands of white intruders from his nation. As a white farmer recalled, "One of our neighbors had refused to pay his permit of $5.00 a year, and this militia, headed by Claude Rainey, came to collect. There were about fifty Indians, some painted, and all having Winchesters and bows and arrows. . . . Needless to say the neighbor handed them his $5.00."[69] In 1881 the Chickasaw government passed another law to protect its public domain: it prohibited the fencing of more than one square mile of land.

Although commercially oriented Chickasaws and intermarried whites denounced Overton (even calling for his impeachment), he enjoyed the majority of the voters' support. He was an unbeatable gubernatorial candidate until his early death by pneumonia at the age of forty-seven in 1884.[70] While Overton was governor and the legislature was dominated by the National Party, the Chickasaws made conditions for whites as unappealing as they could. Overton won federal recognition of the Chickasaws' right to tax and to use force to control U.S. citizens in Indian Territory. Still, the intruder problem only grew worse when the Atchinson, Topeka, and Santa Fe route pushed through the Chickasaw Nation in 1887. As Special Agent John Donaldson reported, "Thousands began to pour in, as the situation was favorable. It cost but a nominal sum to rent valuable farming lands of the Indians, living was cheap, and the return from agricultural labors was large."[71]

Under National Party governor William Byrd's administration (1888–92), the Chickasaw government stepped up its efforts to slow the white intrusion. In 1889 the legislature passed an act authorizing the Chickasaw police to cut wire fences in excess of one mile. A white "boomer," H. F. O'Beirne, noted, "The passage of the act forbidding any more fencing of the common domain for pasturage, and the threatened destruction of all fences outside the limit allowed by law, is unpromising for white settlers."[72] That same year Byrd asked for federal help in removing some six thousand white intruders who refused to pay their permit fees.[73] Byrd's brother-in-law Judge Overton Love, the tribe's official agent in Washington, D.C., warned intruders that a troop of cavalry would march with Byrd's Indians to the homes of every noncitizen, and those unable to produce a permit would be (along with their families) "placed under arrest immediately and hustled out of the country with strict orders not to return." Judge Love stressed that the militia would eject only lawless whites from the nation: "We claim that when the white man comes among us to reside he should obey our laws just as he would have to observe the laws of Texas or any other place where he might live, and we intend he shall obey our laws if he lives in our nation."[74]

The U.S. government's commitment to removing intruders was minimal. U.S. agent Leo Bennet admitted: "When this agency simply threatens and fails to act, as has been the case for years, the trouble will not only continue but increase."[75] When the Department of the Interior finally acted in 1891, it allocated only $100 to finance the expulsion of white intruders. Then the U.S. District Court at Paris, Texas, interfered with Bennet's work by arresting Indian police for "robbing" white men of their revolvers. The same court also refused to issue warrants for the arrest of whites who resisted Indian police officers with shotguns.[76]

White trespassers had so much advance notice in the territorial newspapers that the Indian militia, shored up by U.S. troops, was coming that by the time they set out, the intruders had vacated their homes. A Texas journalist mockingly reported that after two weeks' search, the Indian militia and soldiers "have found a few intruders whom they employed as cooks and teamsters."[77] Governor Byrd experienced such frustration over the ways in which intruders forged permits and evaded his militia he recommended that the legislature repeal the permit law and forbid white settlements altogether. An editor of the *Purcell Register* claimed that the governor was raving mad, determined "that no white man shall remain in his domain under any circumstance."[78]

Another journalist quipped, "The [U.S.] government will probably not again be so ready to lend aid in such a cause."[79] Indeed, the U.S. government ignored the Chickasaws' subsequent calls for help, and whites caught on. Now they generally refused to pay the permit fee or to abide by the laws of the Chickasaw Nation. Zach Redford, who had once paid the permit fees, now refused to do so. He explained that if all the whites decided not to pay it, the militia would have to "move the whole Territory out."[80] He and other whites looked forward to the forcible allotment of Chickasaw lands and statehood.

In 1898 the Curtis Act authorized the secretary of the interior to disband tribal governments and allot tribal lands. The Dawes Commission voided all previous lease contracts between Indians and whites, and ordered white renters off their homesteads. Noncitizen farmers petitioned for an amendment to the Dawes Commission treaty that entitled them to lands. They maintained that "they were there under contract with the individual Indian and that the Indian government has encouraged them to come there and enter into these contracts . . . and that under these contracts the Chickasaw nation has developed. There have been houses built, farms opened up, schools and churches built, and Indians have derived a large annual revenue from them."[81]

Commissioner Henry Dawes sympathized with whites dislodged by allotment policy and prepared a town-site bill to give whites ownership of the lots they had developed. Few Chickasaws settled in railroad towns, which were almost all-white communities. Dawes failed to secure the consent of the Chickasaws and other Five Tribes for this bill; in fact, the Chickasaw government sent delegates to Washington to fight it. Dawes reported that the tribal government "insisted that under no conditions would a United States citizen be permitted to gain title to any portion of the national soil no matter what amount of capital or other improvement he had been invited or permitted to invest."[82]

Despite Chickasaw opposition, the Dawes Commission segregated town-sites from allotment. Whites gained the right to compensation for their improvements and to bid first on the lands that they had improved. This led to speculation in Chickasaw allotments. After Chickasaw allottees sold occupancy rights to noncitizens, they erected some kind of building that they could call an improvement in order to claim the right to buy the lot at a reduced price. In the interest of rapid economic progress, U.S. judges allowed this practice, ruling that Indian allottees could rent for any purpose.[83]

In 1903, after allotment opened the Chickasaws' lands to whites, the problem of white intrusion worsened. The *New York Times* reported: "There are on average over 2,000 complaints every year from the Five Tribes against the refusal of lessees to pay rent or to get off the Indians' lands." The Dawes Commission had agreed to "put each allottee in possession of his land and to remove all objectionable persons from it. In practice this was never done."[84] The magnitude of the task required a concerted effort on the part of the U.S. government, which was lacking. On the Chickasaws' tillable land, there were a hundred white people to the square mile who would have to be moved to put the Indian in possession of his allotment.

Sometimes Chickasaw individuals resisted other Chickasaws' occupation of their property. For as long as possible, intermarried white rancher William Washington prevented Chickasaw allottees from settling on his range. White settler Jake Williams maintained that when Indian claimants attempted to "move in and stretch a tent or build a little shack on Washington's pasture, Washington's men would go out at night, bundle up their belongings, hog-tie them, carry them to the edge of the pasture and throw them out." Finally, the cattle king "took his outfit and moved to New Mexico."[85]

In sum, the Chickasaw Nation successfully defended its legal right to tax white immigrants in U.S. courts, but it won the right too late and lacked the means to enforce it. By that time, whites looked forward to the time when the Chickasaw government would be abolished, Chickasaw lands partitioned and opened to white settlement. Governor Overton's fear that the influx of whites would undermine his nation's sovereignty was fully warranted. Whites, some of them Chickasaws by marriage, pressed Washington to end the Chickasaws' tribal government and system of land tenure.[86]

One of the greatest threats to Chickasaw sovereignty was internal, as some members put immediate personal gain ahead of the common interest of the tribe as a whole. Overton warned them that their dreams of profit under the new regime were illusory. While their rights under the sovereign Chickasaw Nation had made them wealthy, white newcomers would defraud them of most of their gains after Oklahoma statehood.[87] As Overton had prophesied, allotment and statehood did not enrich the Chickasaws. Nor did it turn Chickasaw ranchers into successful farmers, as Commissioner Dawes had said it would. Instead, it resulted in the transfer of most of the Chickasaws' lands and mineral resources from Indians to whites. Government agencies and white-owned businesses discriminated against Indian farmers.[88] While taxation had been employed over many years in the late nineteenth century to preserve Chickasaw autonomy, ultimately this effort to retain tribal land and Chickasaw political authority failed.

5
Curbing the Influence of Intermarried White Men, 1870s–1907

The Chickasaws sought to retain their political autonomy and control of tribal lands in a number of ways. They sought these goals in their relations with the western tribes, in their handling of freedpeople, and in their attempt to regulate their citizens' marriages with whites. The issue of intermarriage confronted the Chickasaws with a major dilemma related to the control and retention of their tribal lands. While the Chickasaws encouraged intermarriage with whites, some designing men and women married Chickasaws to gain admittance to the tribal rolls, with all the rights and privileges of citizenship. The Chickasaw Nation's large landholdings and small number of citizens made membership more valuable than in any of the other Five Tribes.

In most cases, it was white men who intermarried with Chickasaw women, only seeking Indian lands and often abandoning their Indian wives soon after marriage. On the other hand, many marriages were successful and the whites were valuable supporters of the tribe. According rights to white advocates seemed to serve the interests of the tribe. Granting similar rights to the opportunists was not at all in the interest of the Chickasaw Nation. The law required consistency, but how to grant rights to some intermarried whites but not to others became a very difficult problem for the Chickasaws.

Under the communal landholding system, the Chickasaws, like the other members of the Five Civilized Tribes, developed a considerable livestock industry. Because the Chickasaws' range was public domain, prospective Chickasaw ranchers needed only to occupy land with their herds to establish grazing rights. After the Civil War ended, the booming cattle industry attracted white immigrants to the Chickasaw Nation, some of them as legal residents through their intermarriage to Chickasaw women. By 1890 the Chickasaw Nation included about a thousand intermarried whites; of these, about one-third had obtained marriage licenses from the nation, thereby acquiring Chickasaw citizenship and, for a time, the right to vote, hold office, and share in the profits from the leasing and sale of tribally owned lands.[1]

Prior to Indian Removal, the Chickasaws had adopted whites, predominantly men, with whom their people intermarried. They enjoyed the general protection of the tribe and their spouse's relatives, but were not usually adopted by a specific clan. The Chickasaw Nation's marriage pool was limited, and their incest rules were stricter than those of white Americans. The Chickasaws could not marry anyone from their mother's clan (there were seven major clans), and they welcomed educated outsiders.

From the start, the introduction of white men into the Chickasaw population presented both problems and opportunities. In the second half of the eighteenth century, Americans introduced African slaves and plantation agriculture to Chickasaw society. Some white men taught their Chickasaw children English and materialistic cultural values, and occasionally even sent them out of the nation to American schools and left them all their property in American-style wills. The problem was not the ill intent of the white men but rather the force of American law. U.S. courts refused to accept Chickasaw matrilineal definitions of married women's rights. If the United States recognized the legitimacy of the match, it followed the laws governing women in the States. This left Chickasaw women married to U.S. citizens vulnerable. One case in 1837 involved a Chickasaw woman who had married an American soldier but lived separately from him. After vandals robbed her home, she tried to sue them in court. The Arkansas judge refused to hear her case on the grounds that as a wife of a U.S. citizen, her property belonged to her husband, no matter how she obtained it, and *he* would have to sue for its recovery.[2]

During the Chickasaws' relocation to Indian Territory, intermarried whites had received monies from the sale of the Chickasaws' Mississippi homeland. After the Indian Removal, the Chickasaws had incorporated whites into their nation with full privileges and the status of citizenship. Under the constitution of 1856, the Chickasaw Nation formally adopted intermarried whites. The tribe granted them access to national funds and the elective franchise, although this was not spelled out in the constitution. (In contrast, the constitution specifically excluded the Shawnee and Choctaw residents of the Chickasaw district from the right to vote or share in the distribution of national funds.)

Chickasaw women married to whites continued to be vulnerable under federal law, despite tribal efforts to protect them. When a childless Chickasaw woman's white husband died in 1859, her deceased husband's relatives took all his (and her) personal property. Although the Indian agent regretted such incidents, he lacked the power to override the U.S. court system.[3] The federal government rejected the Chickasaws' request that whites who sought Chickasaw citizenship be subjected to their inheritance laws and tried by their courts in the same way native Chickasaws were.

Some intermarried whites, especially those who joined the Chickasaw Nation prior to 1870, identified with tribal interests. They helped the Chickasaws draw up their constitution, and they served as county justices to enforce the new laws. They were active in promoting and running Chickasaw schools. These men usually obeyed the Chickasaws' laws because they respected the tribe, and they benefited from free lands, annuities, and the absence of taxes.[4] Beginning in the 1870s, however, whites in the surrounding states of Texas, Arkansas, and Kansas jealously eyed the Indians' grasslands and sought marriages of convenience with Chickasaw women.[5] A growing number of white men abused the Chickasaws' easy adoption policy in order to enlarge their range and lay claim to a share of Chickasaw national funds.

Not only did the newcomers exploit the nation's common resources for their own personal benefit, they also lobbied for tribal and federal legislation that facilitated their own accumulation of wealth. Freedman Thomas Randolph maintained, "Squaw men as they are called here that is the men that has married chicksaw women run this country if they do not directly they do indirectly."[6] Such men were growing politically powerful and shaping the nation's course in ways that were undesirable to most Chickasaws by blood.

In response to whites' growing dominance over Chickasaw politics and lands, the Chickasaws forged a political party called the National Party that dominated their tribal government in the last quarter of the nineteenth century. Historian Erik Zissu notes that a similar political trend typified each of the Five Tribes, wherein "small farmers rallied political support to preserve Indian dominance over whites."[7] The self-styled Nationalists enacted laws aimed at discouraging whites from seeking citizenship, such as increased marriage license fees, and they eventually disenfranchised white voters.

In the 1870s the Chickasaw government cracked down on "immigration marriages." Chickasaw governor Cyrus Harris blasted the liberal Chickasaw marriage laws that enabled white men to arrange temporary marriages to gain "a foot-hold in the Nation, caring but little for the women whom they take for wives."[8] He denounced the "easy matter of procuring a divorce by mutual consent" and asked the legislature to repeal the law that authorized divorce on any grounds. At Harris's urging, a new law was passed stipulating that any white man or woman who married a Chickasaw Indian and later secured a divorce (except on the grounds of adultery) forfeited access to Chickasaw annuities and lands.[9] Harris's act upheld the rights of long-standing white spouses.

The Chickasaws continued to recognize as fellow citizens valued adopted whites, such as William Jackson. Born in Tennessee, Jackson secured his position of growing prominence in the nation by marrying Chickasaw Anna Donovan and raising nine Chickasaw children to adulthood. During this time, he served as school superintendent, judge, attorney general, and legislator.[10] In an address to the Chickasaw people, Jackson reassured them that "he was and always had been opposed to any change [allotment] . . . he had a Chickasaw wife and nine children and . . . as a man [who] loved his wife and children he would oppose every change."[11] (Jackson himself protested Overton's permit law. So even he favored Chickasaw laws that promoted his personal interests before the tribe's.)

Jackson, however, was not representative of the more recent collection of white immigrants to the Chickasaw Nation, whose commitment to both the marital and the tribal union was weak at best. The quality of intermarried whites declined, as many "loafers and idlers" entered the nation. Worst of all, as historian W. David Baird noted, the new residents "acted as if they were permanent citizens, ignored and segregated the out-numbered Indians, and refused to be bound by law."[12]

With an eye toward improving the quality of intermarried whites, the Chickasaw legislature passed a law in 1876 that required noncitizens to remain in the Chickasaw Nation for a period of two years before they could procure a license to marry a Chickasaw citizen. Before obtaining a marriage license, the noncitizen needed the recommendation of five responsible citizens attesting to his or her good moral character and industrious habits. An official marriage license conferred full rights of membership in the tribe for as long as the marriage bonds endured. In the case of a divorce, the white person lost his rights and privileges.[13]

Another provision of the law specifically discouraged poor whites from intermarrying with Chickasaw women. It stipulated that noncitizens pay $50 for a marriage license. Chickasaw governor Benjamin Overton said that he wanted to put an end to the "mixing of the lowest white blood with the Indian."[14] Despite the stricter 1872 and 1876 marriage laws, white ranchers continued to seek bargain rangeland by means of marriage to Chickasaw women. Spread by newspapers and word of mouth, rumors circulated about the easy wealth to be had through marriage to a Chickasaw or Choctaw woman. Consider a note that a preacher wrote to the head of the Choctaw Nation: "I understand that your tribe offered an inducement in money and land to good moral white men that would marry your young maidens. If this be true, write me at once and I will come. I also will furnish all references." Similarly, a Texan rancher sent an inquiry to the Chickasaw legislature about potential brides. He explained that he "wanted to marry an Indian girl so he wouldn't have to pay the permit on a large herd of cattle."[15]

A couple of incidents illustrate Chickasaw families' objections to such marriages. One Chickasaw father took a justice of the peace to court for marrying his underage daughter to a white man without his or his wife's consent. "I would not have let him come in my yard," the father said.[16] In another case, a daughter from the McGloflin family wanted no part of marriage to a white suitor from the Rimsley family. After the girl rejected him, Rimsley continued to harass her and her family. One day he boasted that he "did not care anything about any d——d Indian anyhow," and challenged her brother to a duel. That evening the girl's brother and a friend allegedly killed Rimsley.[17] Rimsley's was not the only violent death of a white who sought intermarriage. Right after the death of Indian rancher Cubby Cutch, Jess Brown married his widow. When the newlywed Brown began collecting his wife's cattle from the range, unnamed Chickasaws shot him. It is likely that the woman's or Cutch's relatives believed that Brown had exploited her for her wealth.[18] In still other cases, whites "seduced" Indian women and the girls married them to escape shame.

Chickasaw women's stories of neglect and abuse were common. In testimony taken during Chickasaw-Choctaw citizenship hearings, Chickasaw women in unhappy marriages with whites described their experiences. Eliza Passmore testified that her husband and his family had mistreated her: "They cut off her hair to disfigure her and did everything to make it unpleasant for her to stay." Eliza insisted that she did not reject her husband because he was white and lived with white folks (as he maintained). She divorced him "because he did not care for her and . . . he did not marry her in good faith and . . . he did not truly treat her as his wife."[19]

Abandonment was the most common complaint of Chickasaw women. Sara Burns recalled that "sometimes the men would not live with these Indian girls after they got their land." Another Chickasaw woman told the court, "I just don't remember what his name was I didn't get very well acquainted with him, we were just married for one night."[20] Shortly after his marriage, a rancher named Joins put his Chickasaw wife in a hotel, saying that he would not "live with a Damned Indian." He told neighbors that he "never intended to live with [his Indian wife] though he would see that she was always provided for."[21] Another intermarried white, who had separated from his Chickasaw wife, bragged that the "Chickasaws had laws by which they married the whites but there was no law to make them live together."[22] This was the impression given by American newspapers. As a *New York Times* journalist noted of white cattlemen married to Indian women: "While they keep their herds in the Territory they keep themselves in Texas or Kansas."[23]

One finds other accounts of unhappy marriages based on convenience in the WPA narratives. A Texan came to white resident Frank Wright's farm inquiring where he could find Indian girls. He wanted to marry one so he would not have to pay the permit on a large herd of cattle. His friend offered to introduce him to some mixed-blood Chickasaw girls, but he said he had no time for courting and wanted a girl who would marry him right away. He found a Chickasaw woman who married him the same day. Not surprisingly, their marriage failed. Although her white husband reportedly "bought the girl anything she wanted and was as good to her as he could be," an onlooker observed that "she couldn't be happy away from her own people . . . it was very difficult for [Indian women] to break their home ties."[24] Pioneers recalled that Indians tended to live in small settlements apart from white railroad towns and ranching communities.[25] She was surely not the only homesick wife who left her white husband's isolated ranch to return to her family. According to some reports, cattlemen in a hurry pursued women of full Indian descent in order to sidestep the longer courtship period demanded by affluent white and bicultural Chickasaw fathers. The language barrier and cultural conflicts were intensified in such hastily conducted marriages.

In seeking separations from their white husbands, Chickasaw women rarely provided examples of the subtle misunderstandings that may have led to larger quarrels. Many accounts indicate that whites in general ridiculed traditional Chickasaw customs that persisted well into the nineteenth century and beyond. It may not be too much of a stretch to assume that white rancher husbands also derided or opposed their Chickasaw wives' participation in some of them. So many whites mocked Indian funeral "cries" that some Indians ceased the custom and others kept what used to be a public event as private as possible.[26] At a "Cry," Chickasaws gathered and cried over the graves of their ancestors. They stayed until the food they had brought held out, sometimes for a week.[27]

Similarly, white ranchers might have opposed their wives' burying valued goods with deceased family members. A white settler recalled that one Chickasaw woman "poured an apron full of gold and silver over [her] child's grave. This was to tell the Great Spirit how much they valued the child."[28] A white farmer who doubled as a coffin maker recalled that many Chickasaws buried their dead under the floors of their cabins instead of in cemeteries.[29]

The Chickasaw custom that most gained white notice was the pashofa dance for the sick. Dr. J. H. Blackburn, a white doctor, noted that he "was never called on by any of the fullblood Indians . . . they had their medicine man, and when one was sick, they would have a sick dance and drive the evil spirits away."[30] One white pioneer described the ritual she had attended on a number of occasions: "A big fire was made and the patient was laid nearby but they had guards to stand by to see that nothing passed between the fire and the patient, not even a dog. The fire was supposed to be burning up the evil spirit. The Indians would then form in several circles and dance. When the dance was over they would have a big pot of Tom Fuller (hominy) to eat."[31]

Intermarried whites frequently boasted that they were interested in nothing more than securing the right to rangeland through marriage to a Chickasaw woman. Henry Tussey, who owned one of the largest ranching outfits in Indian Territory, admitted that he and other men "married Indians so we could stay here."[32] Some cattlemen testified that their Chickasaw wives "understood all the time that the matter was merely a money matter."[33] Chickasaw Patty Hall reportedly married several white men successively, giving each of them citizenship privileges, and was paid for her trouble. Chickasaw Jim Gibson accepted $100 to persuade his granddaughter Eliza to marry a white rancher. The stockman "had over two thousand head of cattle and they were about losing that cattle" when he stuck this deal with Gibson.[34]

While some Chickasaw women welcomed the prestige and financial security that came from being a white rancher's wife, others found the business-oriented proposals of white cattlemen insulting. Minnie Leftwich's first proposal of marriage confirmed her fears that men would seek her hand in order to obtain a "headright." She was appalled when a prosperous Texas cattleman proposed that they get married because "you have the land. I have the cattle."[35]

Although less is said in the records about white women as opportunistic marriage partners, we find several cases in which prominent Chickasaw cattlemen married white women to cement business partnerships with white ranchers. Chickasaw authorities summoned Chickasaw Alfred Murray to trial for grazing the stock of his father-in-law, a Texas cattleman named Carr. Likewise, Chickasaw Jim Gains reportedly held cattle for his father-in-law, stockman Andy Addington, and Chickasaw Edward Burney leased land to his father-in-law, white rancher Joe Cross. These white fathers-in-law were active in building four barbed wire fences for other ranchers. Sometimes enterprising Chickasaw ranchers lacked the technical expertise, funds, or supplies to fence and expand their ranches. Such business interests led several Chickasaw ranchers to marry white women whose families were in the business of ranching or enjoyed political influence at the national level. Although a small minority of Chickasaw families benefited from such marriages of convenience, the nation as a whole paid a steep price for the illicit invasion of whites, their barbed wire, and their large cattle herds.

Intermarried white William Washington adjoined his ranch to the pasture of his brother-in-law, Chickasaw Richard McLish. They built a drift wire fence around both ranches that extended some thirty to forty miles. Cowhand Tom White recalled that the "McLish and Washington cattle ranch was a big affair; they had a hundred chuck wagons, and when they branded calves, they divided them into thirty-three shares. Their mammoth herds grazed over thousands of acres of public domain." When the Indian militia tried to cut Washington's wire fences because their length was in excess of the mile that tribal law allowed, he resisted by force of arms and had his farmhands kill all the militia's horses to prevent it from carrying out its duty. Washington epitomized the worst type of lawless, intermarried citizen.[36]

In 1887 and 1890 the Chickasaw legislature passed tougher marriage laws. With such restrictive legislation, the Chickasaws tried to make conditions for whites as unappealing as they could. However, they could not do this without inadvertently punishing valued white members of the Chickasaw Nation. The new legislation restricted the rights of all white residents, whatever their standing in the community. Plans to make provisions for "the best of them" proved unworkable.[37]

In the Choctaw Nation, the white intrusion elicited a similar response. Governor Coleman Cole declared, "The Choctaw Nation is being filled up with white persons of worthless character by so called marriages to the great injury of the Choctaw people."[38] Under his leadership, in 1878 the Choctaw legislature tried to assure some accountability on the part of white spouses. It passed an intermarriage law demanding that whites seeking Choctaw spouses present recommendations by ten respectable Choctaws, take a vow of loyalty, and pay a $20 marriage license fee.[39] In 1888 the Choctaws raised the license fee to $100, which caused one reporter to remark: "Such a tax proves that the Choctaws (at least) are not overeager for any closer acquaintanceship with the average white man."[40]

The Chickasaws resorted to even more drastic measures. Chickasaw judge Overton Love and Lemuel Reynolds (formerly an opponent of Overton), supporters of narrowly defeated gubernatorial National Party candidate William Byrd, drew up a disfranchisement act in 1887, which stripped intermarried whites of suffrage and officeholding. When intermarried whites held mass conventions at Purcell and Ardmore to protest this abridgement of their rights, Love and Reynolds traveled to Washington to defend the act. The delegates emphasized Chickasaw women's mistreatment. They maintained that many intermarried whites "had either lost their Chickasaw wives and married white women, or abandoned or become divorced from their Chickasaw wives." Thus the Chickasaw legislature had acted in "self-defense" against numerous abuses of Chickasaw women, as well as to protect the Chickasaws' public domain. They stated that they found it "impossible to separate in practice those who, in good faith, maintained the marriage relation, from those who resorted to the marriage ceremony merely as a trick for robbing the Chickasaws of their pasture land."[41]

Intermarried whites and their Chickasaw allies contested the constitutionality of the 1887 disfranchisement act. A reporter for the *Fort Smith Elevator* maintained that "the adopted citizens of the Chickasaw Nation are doing some vigorous kicking over the recent act of the council which disfranchised them."[42] The U.S. attorney general ruled that the Chickasaws had the right to unseat intermarried whites, for they had established a precedent in 1856 when they denied suffrage to Choctaw residents of their country.[43]

Whites continued to run for office (and win), but the Chickasaw legislature refused to seat them. In September 1889, by a vote of 6-4, the Chickasaw legislature unseated Frank Murray, a citizen of the Chickasaw Nation by marriage and a notorious violator of tribal limits on fencing.[44] The legislature ousted Murray on the strength of the U.S. attorney general's decision. At a special election, the Chickasaws replaced Murray with a citizen by blood. Other legislators were unseated, and Medicine Man Falater and Sam Tababy emerged to replace them. The transformation in Chickasaw government extended beyond removing white officeholders and replacing them with Indians. The newly elected officers spoke little English, and national business was conducted primarily in the Chickasaw language.[45]

After the National Party curtailed "white" Chickasaws' political rights, the Progressive Party struggled to restore intermarried whites' participation in the tribal government.[46] In late March 1890, Chickasaw Sam Paul traveled to Washington to lobby for the rights of disfranchised citizens. Paul, whose father was one of the wealthiest ranchers in the nation and a white man, determined to win back the franchise for intermarried whites. White voters could then restore intermarried whites' right to partake of the Chickasaws' national funds—and put Paul in office. In June 1890 Paul announced his decision to run for tribal governor. He wrote to the secretary of the Interior asking that the U.S. government grant adopted Chickasaw citizens the right to vote in tribal elections. He intimated that if the rights of intermarried whites were denied, there would be bloodshed.[47]

The Chickasaw national election of 1890 centered on the future status of intermarried whites. An editor of the *New York Times* explained what was at stake: "The white husbands have too large interests in the farming and cattle business of the Chickasaw Nation to submit to the present decision without a hard struggle."[48] In past years Chickasaw annuities were trifling, but the Chickasaws awaited a much larger annuity. The federal government agreed to pay Choctaw and Chickasaw citizens nearly $3 million for that portion of the Leased District assigned to the Cheyenne and Arapaho Indians.[49] A writer for the *New York Times* noted, "The question as to what constitutes citizenship is all the more important" because of the payouts for the transfer of the Choctaw and Chickasaws' title to the Cheyenne and Arapaho lands.[50] Not only were the Chickasaws reluctant to subdivide payments with intermarried whites, the federal government's determination to allot the Five Tribes' land put ownership of almost 20 million acres and a share of perhaps billions of dollars up for grabs.[51] The Chickasaw Nation wanted to silence the many intermarried whites who agitated for allotment schemes. The most unscrupulous whites hoped to sell their allotments at a profit and then abandon their Indian wives and children.[52]

The electoral contest was so tense between Nationalist candidate William Byrd and Progressive Paul in 1890 that Byrd stationed the Chickasaw militia at the polls, while U.S. marshals were also on hand.[53] The authorities maintained the peace by establishing separate voting places for white Chickasaws. After the election, the Chickasaw legislature called upon the Chickasaw Supreme Court to decide whether or not the intermarried whites were entitled to vote.[54] The Chickasaw court's decision that the disfranchisement act was constitutional assured National Party candidate Byrd's election. The U.S. secretary of the interior upheld the court's decision. Angered by his defeat, Paul again threatened violence: "If the disfranchisement of these people is legal, then there is no law but force in this nation."[55]

After Byrd's victory, the Chickasaw government passed a tougher disfranchisement act. The Act of 1890 put to rest the Progressives' charge that the 1887 legislation, which emerged from a special session, lacked popular support. The act not only disfranchised intermarried whites, it stripped away their property rights. Intermarried whites would have no "right of soil or interest in the vested funds belonging to the Chickasaws, neither the right to vote nor hold any office in this nation." Furthermore, the act deprived intermarried whites who were widowed and remarried to U.S. citizens of their rights to citizenship.[56]

Boomer newspapers predicted that the "tyrannical act" of 1890 would "play an important part in bringing about an entire change of conditions in affairs of the nation."[57] Intermarried whites held meetings and issued warnings that if the Chickasaw government made any attempt to dispossess them, they would "exterminate every member of this council from the Chief down."[58] When a committee representing the disfranchised whites accosted Byrd about the unjustness of the law, he "stated to his white brethren that it was the object of his party to strip them of every vestige of land interest."[59]

Defeated gubernatorial candidate Paul applied for U.S. citizenship, saying he wished to protect his property interests "against hostile legislation from the party in power."[60] Paul wrongly believed that U.S. citizenship would convey him absolute title to a section of Chickasaw lands. Of course, the Chickasaw government was not about to enable its own citizens, the beneficiaries of liberal land laws and national funds, to escape its jurisdiction or subdivide its lands. After Paul became a U.S. citizen, outraged Chickasaw legislators passed the following act: "That whenever any citizen of this nation, whether by birth or adoption or by marriage, shall become a citizen of any nation, or of the United States, or any other government, all his or her rights of citizenship in this nation shall cease, and he or she shall forfeit all rights to land and money belonging to the Chickasaw people." The U.S. attorney general and the secretary of the interior struck down the law, stating that it was "most discreditable to the nation" and that the Chickasaws should make the attainment of U.S. citizenship "the chief object of their elevation and progress."[61]

At this point, the Chickasaw Progressive Party cut its ties with Paul and, further, charged that the "Progressive" boomer newspapers misrepresented it. The party held a convention to clarify its position: "We are opposed to the allotment of land and territorial government and none except a few, some of disappointment, and others from spite, but none of much repute have ignored that platform. That Senator Paul is not considered as the leader . . . nor is he endorsed for taking oath of allegiance to the United States, nor in his suit for lands."[62] The Progressive Party stood for the defense of intermarried Chickasaws' rights but not for the dissolution of the Chickasaw Nation.

Many intermarried whites, but not Chickasaws by blood, favored bills to break up the Chickasaw government and lands. Some believed, like Paul, that statehood would bring them greater security over their property. In 1893 a territorial newspaper expressed this view: "For the past four or five years they have lived in a position of doubt as to their rights and standing in the nation and in constant fear lest some move should be made to take from them all or some part of their property rights. . . . No later than this summer have they stood in trembling expectance, fearing that they were to be denied a share in the leased district money."[63]

Though an exceptional man by all accounts, Paul revealed the extent to which intermarried whites and their family members could exploit tribal privileges for private ends without serious repercussions. When a young Paul shot a white man in the back, the tribal authorities lobbied for and won a presidential pardon for his reckless behavior. He was acting in the role of light-horseman, and it seemed critical to defend the jurisdiction and rights of the Indian police force within the Chickasaw Nation. However, when the Chickasaw government curtailed Paul's political ambitions and attempt to become an urban developer, he turned against the nation, drawing support from Americans who wanted to end Indian sovereignty. His direct calls for the end of "kangaroo Indian governments" proved too much for even his former friends and political supporters in the Chickasaw Nation. Angered Chickasaws shot at him when he lectured on the benefits of allotment and statehood, but all the bullets missed until his son's gunshot finally hit the mark.[64]

Like his public life, Paul's private life revealed his unbridled individualism. Newspaper editor Henry O'Beirne noted that Sam Paul's acquisition of "a large property early in life" led him to extravagance and excess.[65] Even his admirers regretted his hotheaded temper and aggressiveness. All three of Paul's marriages failed and in 1892 he died at the hands of his eldest son, who competed for the affections of Paul's last wife. As a reporter noted, "The killing was the ending of an old feud and was not at all unexpected. In fact, it was to the people of Pauls Valley fully as certain that Joe would kill his father or Sam his son at some time or another as that the sun rose and set."[66]

Although they lost their most vocal Chickasaw advocate, intermarried whites refused to give up their voting privileges in the Chickasaw Nation. In 1894 a reporter for a Kansas newspaper stated that intermarried whites would test their right to vote "on the basis of a property right, the issue involved in the election allotment being one in which the squaw men are vitally interested."[67] The Choctaws had not only disfranchised intermarried whites, they passed legislation denying them a share in tribal funds. The fear that the Chickasaw legislature would follow suit galvanized intermarried whites to demand an end to Chickasaw government.

The Dawes Commission put an end to the intermarried whites' fears of economic loss. They made out well. The commission's mission was to divide the Five Tribes' lands into plots that were to be divided among tribal members. As part of this process, the commission either accepted or rejected applicants for tribal membership based on its requirements, which differed from the Five Tribes' rules. For example, the Chickasaw legislature had ruled that "a white man who secured citizenship through marriage with an Indian would lose such citizenship if the Indian died and the white citizen later married a white person. The commission, however, refused to accept this rule, holding that it was contrary to treaty stipulations which held that all citizens should have equal rights."[68] It denounced Chickasaw laws that disenfranchised whites as confiscation laws.

The Dawes commissioners accepted existing citizenship rolls, prepared by the Indian nations, but were authorized to receive applications from any additional persons claiming rights of citizenship and to determine which applicants were Chickasaw citizens. The commissioners did not want Congress to allow the Five Tribes to reduce "good citizens to beggary."[69] The Chickasaw government (what choice did it have?) agreed that intermarried citizens of the Chickasaw and Choctaw nations would participate upon equal terms with other citizens in the allotment of lands and the distribution of tribal property.

Still, many Chickasaws objected to enrolling intermarried whites on the same rolls as citizens by blood. Like the Choctaws, they turned to blood quantum as a protective mechanism to safeguard their tribal heritage from wrongful claimants. U.S. commissioners remarked that many Indian citizens held that "blood alone constituted a valid claim to citizenship in the several nations, regardless of other qualifications required by treaties, and the constitution."[70] Accordingly, the Chickasaws prepared three separate rolls: Chickasaws by blood, intermarried whites, and freedpeople.

As the Dawes Commission prepared the rolls, the Chickasaw government took the most drastic steps yet to halt intermarriages between whites and Chickasaws. The Chickasaw legislature raised the marriage license fee to exorbitant rates. In 1898 the Chickasaw Council demanded $600 for a marriage license. The next year the legislature raised the fee to $1,000, with the additional stringent requirement of ten witnesses to the good moral character of the applicant. The Chickasaw attorney general said that the high license fee would "prevent designing persons from speculating in the landed rights of the Chickasaw." As historian Michael Lovegrove noted: "With the bill's passage, the Chickasaws did everything legislatively possible to preclude non-citizens from eligibility for allotment of land or any other privileges of citizenship."[71]

Governor Douglas Johnston explained the necessity for the raised marriage license fee: "[T]he immediate allotment of the land and distribution of tribal property has given an impetus to marriages between non-citizens and female citizens of this nation that is both alarming and shocking. It is apparent to those familiar with conditions here that many of these marriages are in utter disregard of the sacred rights of matrimony and are entered into by adventurers of the surrounding states for the sole purpose of sharing in the tribal property."[72]

Governor Johnston explained that marriages were legal without licenses, but it was licenses that conferred citizenship rights: "If the non-citizen procures a license and marries a citizen of this nation according to its laws he may share in the lands and other tribal property." He might secure a wife under U.S. law without purchasing a license, but he would not "share in the property of the tribe as one of its citizens."[73]

County court judges found themselves flooded with requests for marriage licenses. Governor Johnston sent letters to the county judges requesting that they refuse to join any more whites and Chickasaws in matrimony until the U.S. government closed the allotment rolls. A journalist for the *New York Times* reported the trend among all the Five Tribes: "A good many men, some 2,500, married Indian women with all possible rapidity and a good many more discovered Indian blood hitherto unsuspected. Everybody tried to get on the rolls for the distribution."[74] Many long court battles lay ahead before a per capita payment could be made to the nation.

The Chickasaws and Choctaws held lands jointly but conducted separate rolls, and they would not have complete say over who would be counted as citizens of their nations. To the Chickasaws' enrollment of about 4,500 citizens, the Dawes Commission added 334 names (and it added 1,202 Choctaws to the Choctaws' rolls). The corruption came when federal courts of the territory heard appeals on the part of persons refused admission to the rolls and admitted another 728 to the Chickasaws' rolls (and 1,772 to the Choctaws' rolls) without the tribes' input or consent. They were known as "court citizens." Both the tribes and the interested whites hired lawyers and fought a protracted legal battle. Under the Supplementary Agreement of 1902, Congress created the Citizenship Court to hear the Chickasaw and Choctaw nations' appeals against thousands of fraudulent cases. The Chickasaws saved $20 million by disallowing thousands of false claims.[75]

Governor Johnston drafted a conciliatory bill that recognized intermarried citizens' rights as the same as other citizens' and prohibited discriminating against them.[76] By this time, few Chickasaws opposed white suffrage because most of the issues that would determine the nation's future had already been settled. Johnston's act served the dual purpose of securing him white votes and healing Indian-white racial tensions. Johnston's successor, Governor Palmer Moseley (1904–6), applauded Johnston's act as a measure that would promote national unity: "There no longer exists any possibility for a discrimination to be made in the political and property rights of our citizens . . . in the closing years of our national government, all citizens may participate equally and without distinction."[77]

In the end, the Chickasaws paid their lawyers $750,000 to see 2,069 wrongful claimants stricken off the Chickasaw and Choctaw rolls and more than seven hundred pending appeals cases dismissed.[78] In 1910 the Five Tribes petitioned the U.S. government to finally close the rolls, stating that they had already spent $1 million defending themselves against fraudulent claims of citizenship in their nations. They added, "Had the question of deciding on Indian blood been left to the Indian courts, it would have been settled more swiftly and justly."[79]

Political weakness relative to the United States and their own divided sentiments hindered the Chickasaws' efforts to minimize the presence and influence of whites in their nation. Although Chickasaw leaders tried to stem the flood of white immigration, they lacked the necessary U.S. military and judicial support to enforce discriminatory legislation against whites living in their nation. Tribal sentiment toward whites was divided, because many had become integrated into Chickasaw families and communities through marriage. Moreover, white residents of the Chickasaw Nation rallied the sympathy of the American public and government to a far greater extent than Indian or freedpeople claimants to Chickasaw lands and resources did. Clearly, the Chickasaw dilemma in dealing with intermarriage in such a way as to retain tribal lands and limit rights to supporters of the tribe was not effectively resolved.

While having a white spouse may have meant getting ahead economically and socially in American society, it also meant the incorporation of a powerful group of outsiders with a greater allegiance to another government and set of values. Most intermarried whites had little use for Chickasaw laws except as a way to gain access to tribal lands and funds.

Their concomitant citizenship within a dominant political entity made white Chickasaws a dangerous wedge to the extension of American sovereignty over the Chickasaw Nation. They soon found that they could enjoy free lands and other privileges of Chickasaw citizenship while also enjoying relative immunity to the execution of tribal laws, especially those limiting the hoarding of real estate and sale of natural resources found within the bounds of the lands they claimed. When faced with a backlash from angry Chickasaws, intermarried whites clamored for private ownership of the farms and towns they developed.

6
Keeping the School System under Chickasaw Control, 1880–1907

In keeping with the consistent Chickasaw effort to maintain autonomy, at the turn of the twentieth century, the Chickasaw national government resisted the United States' takeover of its separate school system, defended its right to run things its way, and sought to use its funds exclusively for the education of Chickasaws by descent. The other members of the Five Tribes had surrendered their schools earlier, as early as 1899. Chickasaw governor Douglas Johnston recounted: "[The United States] sought control of the Chickasaw schools. We resisted. . . . We were permitted to retain control of our schools until 1906, six years longer than any one of the other Five Civilized Tribes."[1]

Until Oklahoma statehood, the Chickasaws managed their own schools, paid their own expenses, and furnished their own teachers. The Chickasaws held out under conditions that severely tested them because they wanted to maintain their tribal and cultural autonomy. Meanwhile, the United States progressively deprived other Indian tribes of independence and authority and sought to integrate Indian children into mostly white schools.

Just prior to the Civil War, the Chickasaws severed their relationship with missionaries because of the latter's racial prejudice. In 1855 at Wapanucka Academy, a Presbyterian schoolmaster whipped some girls publicly, explaining, "These little rogues need something more than mere kindness to manage them. They are full of evil from the crown of the head to the sole of their feet."[2] The missionaries' prejudice against these girls colored their correspondence. They hated to send the girls home to their "ungodly" parents, where they would be exposed to "dark" influences."[3] One missionary teacher's relations with her pupils were described as "continual warfare."[4] The girls were plagued with homesickness and fevers, and a few ran away and refused to return.

Unsteady attendance exacerbated conflicts between the missionaries and the Chickasaws over financial matters. The Chickasaw Council agreed to pay $75 for every girl who actually attended Wapanucka Academy (about fifty), whereas the American Board demanded compensation for the hundred students the board had "agreed to receive."[5] They also disagreed on the amounts that the Chickasaw Nation and the board had each pledged to pay for Wapanucka Academy's construction and its furnishings. The board refused to donate any further funds toward finishing a building that belonged not to it but to the Chickasaw Nation.[6] Another complaint against the missionaries was that they were proselytizing rather than teaching. Instead of providing students with a solid academic foundation, the missionaries strove only to make the children literate enough to "study the Bible and be converted to Christianity."[7]

In view of the Chickasaws' controversy with the missionaries over finances and the Bible-centered curriculum, the school trustees advocated that the Chickasaw Council "take over the school and plan for its management under private contract," which it did in 1860.[8] Thenceforth the missionaries withdrew from the nation, anticipating that the Chickasaws would fail in their educational endeavors and plead with them to return. The Chickasaws, however, were determined to succeed without them and designed an educational program that was more responsive to local needs than to the missionaries' religious goals.

The Chickasaws also ended their joint education projects with the Choctaws; they had been disappointed in these collaborative educational experiments. Explorer Josiah Gregg explained why Chickasaws were dissatisfied with the Choctaw Academy in Kentucky, which several Chickasaw students had attended prior to Indian Removal: "They said, with apparent justice, that their boys, educated there, forgot all their customs, their language, their relatives, their national attachments; and, in exchange, often acquired indolent and effeminate, if not vicious habits; and were rendered unfit to live among their people, or to earn a maintenance by labor." They concluded that their funds would be employed to better advantage in their own country, where they could extend "the influence of the institutions . . . to all classes."[9]

After the Civil War, the Chickasaws restored and reopened their schools under their own management and the private contract system.[10] Wapanucka was headed by lead teacher Mary [James] Chiffee, who had attended primary school in the Chickasaw Nation and finished her education in the States.[11] According to the Indian agent for the Chickasaws and Choctaws, Wapanucka and the other Chickasaw schools were in a "prosperous condition" and well attended. In 1879 the Chickasaws' lawyer B. F. Grafton praised their schools: "They have organized a complete system of public instruction within the reach of all their families. In addition to their common schools scattered judiciously over the country, they have established an academy or high school in each of the four counties of the nation."[12] The Chickasaws had thirteen neighborhood schools, which were primary day schools, and five academies, which were high schools that boarded children: Rock Academy at Wapanucka (now changed from a girls' to a boys' school), the Orphans' Home at Lebanon, Collins Institute at Stonewall, Harley Institute at Tishomingo, and Bloomfield Academy near Achille.

The Chickasaw Nation developed a comprehensive system for educating its young people, leading from elementary school through college and offering educated youngsters career opportunities in the nation. The Chickasaw approach to the education of its young embodied a remarkable combination of activities designed to foster Indian young people's national allegiance and attachment to the Chickasaws' cultural traditions and government.

The Chickasaws saw their youth as their future leaders and trained professionals—teachers, lawyers, doctors, and politicians.[13] A primary role of the academies was to prepare Chickasaw children to fill important positions in the nation. As such, Chickasaw students never had to do general maintenance work, which was performed by hired laborers, often former slaves or poor whites. Chickasaw academies opened the way to a college education in the United States for some Chickasaw students, such as Baptist preacher Jim Cobb, who performed well. Cobb stated: "The boys in turn were expected to return to the Chickasaw nation after completing their courses in these [American] schools and become the leaders."[14] These young men returned to the nation and were appointed or elected to the nation's most esteemed offices in government and school administration.

In order to overcome Chickasaw children's fears and the language barrier, the Chickasaw government promoted a localized system of bilingual education for elementary students at neighborhood schools. Ideally, the children could live at home with their parents. Rather than acculturation, the Chickasaw neighborhood schools emphasized the basic rudiments of math, history, geography, science, and English. As described by federal officials: "The primary schools are usually located in full-blood communities in the woods, far removed from the influences of civilization. The children in many instances speak Chickasaw entirely and hear nothing else, except during recitation, as many of the teachers address them in that language outside of the schoolroom."[15]

The Chickasaw government maintained that native teachers' understanding of the Choctaw/Chickasaw language facilitated learning. Although Chickasaw teacher Elizabeth Kemp Mead had little formal education, she could communicate with her second grade students, who knew next to no English. Mead wrote, "I could understand the language enough to teach them the meaning [of Chickasaw words] in English."[16] Moreover, the schools helped to preserve the Chickasaw language in the face of the cultural assault against it, as L. L. Sturdivant, a Chickasaw who grew up mainly among white relatives and neighbors, explained. He learned to speak the Chickasaw/Choctaw language in a neighborhood school taught by Choctaw Ebenezer Pitchlynn. Sturdivant noted that he and two other students at the school spoke only English at home: "We wanted to learn to talk the Indian language and the others wanted to learn to speak English, so we all got busy and learned a lot."[17] Assimilated Chickasaws such as Sturdivant, who had lost their native tongue, welcomed the opportunity to learn it at school.

As much as possible, the Chickasaws wanted their children to be educated by native teachers who shared their values and culture as well as their language. Chickasaw Belle Chigley taught in both white and Chickasaw schools and noted her preference for the latter: "The Indians were very easily managed. The discipline was much easier than in a white school. Indian children would 'sull' [sulk] when they became angry instead of plotting little mean things to do as the white children did."[18] The Chickasaws were especially eager to recruit teachers from their own nation and discouraged outsiders from seeking teaching jobs by levying a permit tax on them.[19] The Chickasaws believed that native teachers would treat the children with more kindness than whites did. They would know how to discipline Chickasaw youth without bodily harming them, and they would not discriminate against them. Not all observers were agreed on the desirability of this approach. The U.S. inspector charged that "teachers are led to believe that the permanency of their positions depends on their ability to 'get along easily' with their students."[20] Mr. Woodson, a teacher at Rock Academy, was reputedly fired because he did not "get on well with the boys."[21]

Other nonnative teachers, principals, and superintendents backed off from conflict with their students that stemmed from cultural differences. A white principal related his futile attempt to discipline a "full-blood" Chickasaw for skipping his oration: "On inquiry I found that he had gone to his room to sulk—refusing to recite. I went up to bring him down. Jesse James, half-blood, followed me and said, 'Mr. Principal, he is a full-blood, he had made up his mind—you might kill him, but he will not come down!' Realizing that I was coping with a fundamental characteristic, I turned and went back downstairs."[22] The principal interpreted this behavioral pattern, as all other "peculiarities" of Chickasaw children, as a racial rather than a cultural trait. He noted, for example, that "the higher the percentage of Indian blood the better artists they were." In praise of his Indian pupils, the principal remarked on "their high regard for truth, their code of honor and their natural oratorical style."[23] This particular white principal understood the cultural divide and was admiring of Chickasaw cultural traits, even if he was guilty of stereotyping.

Less impressed by racial stereotypes, Chickasaw teachers could better understand family circumstances and other personal issues that might distract students from their studies. The chief problem that teachers faced was sporadic attendance because of the observance of mourning rituals, poverty, family problems, and matters that required the children's temporary absence from school. Parents occasionally removed students from the academies "to pick cotton, gather crops, or to take care of the babies."[24] One boy wrote a letter to Superintendent William Jackson explaining that he had been homesick, "wanting to see his brother and sister so bad."[25] Such problems were lessened by the localized setting of neighborhood schools.

The Chickasaws placed a premium on the education of their children because of the momentous challenge that lay ahead. An alumnus of Colbert neighborhood school recalled Choctaw chief George W. Harkin's (1810–90) talk to his class. Harkin reportedly told them that after the trains came, "[p]eople would come in here from everywhere, and if we were not prepared to care for ourselves, they would knock the dirt from under our feet."[26]

While ostensibly aimed at acculturating their students so that they could succeed in white society, Chickasaw academies inculcated national pride in their students; this was their imperative, often emphasized by governors in their inaugural addresses. For example, in 1883 Governor Benjamin Overton emphasized not just the importance of high-quality academics, but also the civic function of the schools: "The moral training of our young men is a subject of the gravest importance to us. They constitute our future hope. By them our churches, schools, laws, and government must soon be administered."[27] He placed an equal stress on young women's education, emphasizing their role as mothers of future tribal leaders.

The letters (1896–97) of Hart Maxcy Smith, a white missionary teacher at Rock Academy, one of the Chickasaws' male academies, reveal that the academy instilled Chickasaw patriotism in its students. In fact, a vital part of the students' education was civic in nature and included visits by leading men of the nation as well as outings to national conventions, where the speakers discussed strategies to defend tribal institutions. They urged the students in their audiences to apply themselves for the good of their nation.[28] After school examinations ended, Indian leaders addressed the hundreds of assembled students and parents. Chickasaw legislator Jesse Bell gave a talk admonishing the children that in a few years time "they would have to protect their tribal rights under treaties with the Federal Government and to compete with educated, sagacious and unscrupulous white men."[29] He was right. The following years saw congressional efforts to dissolve the Chickasaws' government and take over management of their school system.

Smith described a joint Chickasaw-Choctaw convention that he and his students attended: "They reserved seats for us and appointed several orators especially to address the students." The leaders opened the convention by "reading from the Choctaw Bible, singing a hymn in Choctaw and prayer." Most of the addresses were in Chickasaw or Choctaw, but Rock Academy principal William Jackson, an intermarried white, made a speech expressing his opposition to Dawes's allotment policy (a plan to divide and privatize the Indians' communal lands) in English, which was translated into Choctaw by school trustee Lyman Worcester. For almost three hours, Jackson summarized treaty relations between the Indians and the U.S. government, and then closed his speech with "a powerful appeal not to consent to the opening up of the Indian Territory to settlement." Other speeches by other prominent Chickasaw and Choctaw leaders followed. Elder E. C. Jackson, considered the best orator of the Choctaw Nation, "told of things that happened as far back as 1833." After the speeches, the delegates sang, shook hands, and ended the convention with a prayer.[30] After attending this meeting, the students returned to school fired with enthusiasm. Smith recorded how students Ben Greenwood, Will Duncan, and others imitated the convention:

> In the room next to mine the boys were having a meeting last night and the way in which they "took off" what they have heard and seen in public assemblies was quite amusing. I heard one of them get up and say, "Mr. Greenwood, won't you come to the front, sir, and speak a few words of encouragement to us." One of the others interpreted this into Chickasaw and Ben Greenwood got up and said something in Chickasaw, which, of course, I did not understand. Then "Mr. Duncan, we would be glad if you would come up on the stage and give us some good advice." Will Duncan rises, "I would like very much to address you and I had much to say to-

night, but I have such a bad sore throat that I cannot speak." A little later—"I see a fine looking gentleman over there. He looks like he could talk well . . . etc, etc."[31]

From Smith's letters, we see how the boys were groomed for leadership, their self-confidence enhanced by the great attention paid to them by their most respected officials. While the Chickasaw boarding schools promoted assimilation, they also taught their students to respect their leadership and venerate their forefathers.

Smith observed that outside of the classroom, his Rock Academy scholars preferred speaking their own language to English: "The boys here speak english very well but I am told when they talk among themselves always use Chickasaw."[32] Smith also noted that he heard the boys singing in their rooms in the Chickasaw tongue. The fact that Smith picked up Chickasaw words himself and began using them in letters home to his parents affirms the frequency with which the boys spoke Chickasaw at the school. Even Chickasaw academies for older students, where a greater stress was placed on acculturation, reinforced their native language. The students were all Chickasaws, and the schools were situated in Chickasaw communities.

Chickasaw families needed financial support. Smith found it hard to believe that some parents withdrew their children from Rock Academy because of financial necessity: "Some of them actually say that they are not financially able to send their children to school! And sending children to school here means to place them where everything, even their books, is furnished at the expense of the Nation."[33] However, Smith later realized that some boys were taken away "because they were afraid they would not have a new suit for the examination."[34] In his 1897 annual address Chickasaw governor Robert Harris declared, "Many children are kept away from school" because their parents "are not able financially to furnish their children with necessary clothing that they would wish them to have." Even though outsiders thought Chickasaw expenditures "extravagantly expensive," it was not enough for some families.[35]

Paying board money to Chickasaw families was a way to equalize students' access to education by helping to make it affordable for all parents to send their children to school. It was also a way to commit families to the educational process. The Chickasaw government paid parents $10 per month, per child for board, as long as their children attended school. Students who missed more than fifteen consecutive days lost their place in school, and their parents lost the government funds. The government required teachers to make an annual report of attendance, deaths, and "quits," which the national clerk read aloud to the legislature.[36] Chickasaw academies "made expulsion the punishment for going off [the campus] without permission." Students who ran away in the fall semester could not resume classes after winter break.[37] All these points contributed to the Chickasaws' successful efforts to improve school attendance. Most important, the payment of board to Chickasaw parents helped to assure the success of the tribe's educational programs by giving even very poor Chickasaw families a stake in helping to assure the implementation of Chickasaw academic goals and the preservation of tribal culture.

Chickasaw education, in all respects, was designed to benefit the Chickasaws. The schools spread national funds widely throughout the Chickasaw population. By bringing schools to neighborhoods, compensating parents for their children's board, and excluding white students from attendance, Chickasaw leaders mollified members of the nation who were suspicious of whites. The government paid the expenses of accomplished male students who chose to attend American academies and colleges.[38]

Federal critics who arrived in the nation bent on terminating tribal government and schools looked at the Chickasaws' educational system with cultural blinders on. First of all, they saw that it was expensive and sought to trim it down to its bare necessities. Although the Chickasaws had only a quarter of the population of the neighboring Choctaw Nation, the Chickasaw government spent more than twice as much annually on education. It applied the interest on all its funds held by the federal government to education, which amounted to $95,000 annually for approximately eight hundred Chickasaw scholars in the year 1891.[39] To U.S. critics of the Chickasaw schools, the policy of paying children's parents for their board was "extravagantly expensive." The real problem with this policy from the federal government's vantage point was that the money went to Indians and not whites. Under Chickasaw

law, white noncitizens could not board Indian children and were denied compensation for boarding students. Whites petitioned Washington officials when the Chickasaws refused "to pay certain persons who
have, in good faith, boarded and cared for Chickasaw pupils."[40] (Although the Chickasaw government tried to accommodate all families,
some lived in isolated, rural areas, too far from neighborhood schools
to board with their parents.)

In addition, the U.S. inspector for Indian Territory railed against bilingual education. In particular, he alleged that in the neighborhood
schools, Chickasaw teachers discouraged the use of English "by con-
versing with [children] in their own dialect." The Chickasaw government resoundingly denied the charge that bilingual education impeded
its people's advancement and expressed grave concerns about how "full-
blood" Indians could succeed in classrooms geared to the education of
native English speakers.[41] The investment paid off. By 1880 the Chickasaws had achieved the highest literacy rate of all the Indian nations in
Indian Territory. About thirty-six hundred of six thousand Chickasaws
could read and write in English.[42]

In federally run Indian boarding schools, the U.S. policy was to strip
Indian children of their Indian heritage in order to "save" them. Indian students were separated from their relatives and strictly forbidden
to use their native languages, to the point where violators of the rule
were beaten, deprived of food, or put in solitary confinement. In their
defense of bilingual neighborhood schools taught and administered by
Indians, Chickasaw national and school leaders ran counter to the U.S.
campaign to undermine Indian traditions and culture. In 1889 commissioner of Indian Affairs Thomas J. Morgan declared that the Chickasaws were "destined to become absorbed into the national life, not as
Indians, but as Americans."[43]

In response to the meddling of outsiders, the Chickasaw government
reasserted its sole jurisdiction over teacher selection. It passed a law ex-
plicitly stating that "school teachers who may wish to teach school in
this nation shall *not* be required to undergo an examination as to his
or her qualifications, as a teacher, before being permitted to teach such
school."[44] The jewels of the Chickasaw Nation, graduates of Bloomfield
Academy were "immediately considered eligible to teach at any Chicka-

saw schools."[45] Given the reality that opportunities even for educated Indians were frequently circumscribed, teaching positions represented one of the best paths for the advancement of capable Indian students.

Although the Chickasaws had standards for teachers, they did not want their teachers subjected to outsiders' scrutiny. On the surface, WPA interviews with Chickasaw teachers give the impression that requirements for teaching in the neighborhood schools were minimal. Chickasaw Elizabeth Kemp Mead described the "test" that qualified her to teach fourth graders: "There was an arithmetic lying on the table. [The national superintendent] picked it up and said, 'Solve this problem.' I did. Then he took a speech out of his pocket from Gen. Cooper and he said, 'See if you can read this.' I did."[46] Factors that Mead may have overlooked that operated in her favor at the interview were the influence and stature of the Kemp family in the Chickasaw Nation.

Due to the Chickasaws' recruitment efforts, the U.S. superintendent of education, Charles D. Carter, reported, for the school term of 1896–97, there were twelve teachers (out of about twenty) who were "Chickasaws by blood" teaching in the nation's schools.[47] Like the Chickasaws, the other Five Tribes nations preferred native teachers. In 1872 the Cherokee schools boasted that three-fourths of their teachers were Cherokee, and in the Choctaws' schools, half of the teachers were "natives."[48]

In the view of U.S. officials, the presence of Indian teachers was not a sign of Indian progress, but a sign that Chickasaw schools needed reform. Superintendent Carter demanded the dismissal of teachers of Chickasaw ancestry on the grounds that they lacked "special training for their work."[49] When his call for the resignations of Indian teachers went unheeded, Carter pressed each of the Five Tribes to establish some type of summer school program for teachers. In the Cherokee, Choctaw, and Creek nations, the "summer normal" became the regular certifying agency for all teachers. Eventually, at the turn of the century, the Chickasaws set up their own examinations, independent of federal administration.[50]

Likewise, Superintendent Carter scrutinized the character of Chickasaw school superintendents. It was the responsibility of school superintendents to maintain the schools, to keep them filled to capacity, and to choose which students from the academies would go on to colleges in the States. Because of their high public profile as orators at school openings and closings, school administrators' positions were often political stepping-stones. Hundreds of parents and all the important Chickasaw officials attended the academies' closing exercises. School superintendents like Douglas Johnston, William Byrd, Palmer Mosley, and Richard McLish went on to become high officials, even governors (or gubernatorial candidates).[51] Since no other institution commanded as much respect or interest as the schools, Chickasaw law barred noncitizens from the post of school superintendent. Intermarried whites could and did serve as superintendents, but outsiders could not.

This rule of exclusion went back to Governor Benjamin Overton's firing of the white principal of the Orphan's Home, the Reverend D. H. Saunders, in 1881. Saunders had more than $50,000 invested in speculative interests in Indian lands and was an active proponent of opening Indian Territory to white settlement. These facts alone angered Overton, but it was Saunders's sexual misconduct that led to his dismissal. One female student in her teens said that the reverend came to her bed in the middle of the night and offered her money to sleep with him. Some Chickasaws, probably the girl's relatives, made a botched attempt to assassinate him. After driving Saunders from the Chickasaw Nation, Overton strongly recommended that henceforth the legislature appoint only Chickasaw citizens for the important offices of school principals or superintendents.[52] Although Saunders's name was cleared in federal court, it was never cleared in the Chickasaw Nation. At least one other woman, not a student, similarly accused Saunders of an attempt at "seduction."[53] Henceforth, the Chickasaws would entrust their girls and boys only to respected Chickasaw leaders.

The greatest challenge to the Chickasaws' control over their schools came in 1898 when Congress passed the Curtis Act. A monumental blow to the Five Tribes' autonomy, the Curtis Act ended tribal sovereignty, tribal courts, tribal laws, and scheduled tribal governments to terminate on March 4, 1906. It dissolved the Five Tribes' communal land base, providing for its allotment to individuals, reserving coal, asphalt, timberlands, and town sites for sale. Mineral royalties were to be used to support Indian schools. The secretary of the interior, Ethan Allen Hitchcock, had control of these funds and attempted to use his purse power to remake Indian schools into schools for white children. Under the Curtis Act, Congress provided that the governance of Indian Territory schools should pass to the federal superintendent and subordinate supervisors.

After Congress passed the Curtis Act, the Department of the Interior ruled that the Chickasaws and Choctaws must accept a supervisor of education, whose salary should be paid out of the mineral royalty fund, which was made the school fund for the education of Chickasaw and Choctaw children. The Chickasaws claimed the right to supervise their own schools and "the ability to conduct them as they should be conducted." Whereas the Choctaws finally accepted the supervisor, the Chickasaws asserted that the salary of the federal supervisor was an unnecessary expense and they refused to recognize him in an official capacity.[54]

Governor Douglas Johnston denied that the Chickasaws had conceded the right of control to the federal government. "There is no provision for the uprooting and eliminating [of] our system of education; there is no provision for the discharge of our teachers and the hiring of others."[55] What was the justification for an arbitrary act that wrested from the Chickasaws management and control of their cherished institutions?

Not only did Secretary Hitchcock take control of the schools without their consent, he chose the imperious John D. Benedict as the first federally appointed superintendent of Indian Territory schools. Benedict thought little of Indians and even less of their schools. For the most part, Benedict's criticisms of Chickasaw schools reflected his racist beliefs that Indians were unfit for higher education, their language and culture were inferior, and their most successful leaders were unqualified to teach in and manage schools. Governor Johnston dismissed Benedict's criticisms of his native teachers, bilingualism, and "extravagance" out of hand. He did not care how Chickasaw schools "compared to systems of education in vogue elsewhere" and asked only that if whites visited Chickasaw schools and found something to praise, they acknowledge it.[56]

All the Five Tribes except the Chickasaws turned over their schools to Benedict because he controlled their national funds and their mineral royalties, but Governor Johnston would not budge. When Benedict refused to hand over the Chickasaws' share of the coal and asphalt royalties, which were jointly owned with the Choctaws, Johnston hired lawyers to challenge the Department of the Interior's right to withhold their funds until the Chickasaws submitted to federal authority. (Secretary Hitchcock later charged Governor Johnston with financial impropriety because he spent national funds on this legal effort).[57]

Benedict's underling, John M. Simpson, the federal supervisor for Chickasaw education, failed to secure Governor Johnston's support for his teacher examinations. In 1898 Simpson reported, "I do not believe the Chickasaw schools would participate in a summer normal. They constitute a very headstrong bunch and have their own ideas about things."[58] Indeed, the Chickasaws remained deeply committed to their own academic goals and objectives. After much quarreling with Chickasaw leaders, Simpson announced that he would not attempt to hold a normal in their nation and resigned from the Indian Service. The Chickasaws took the initiative and held their own normal, which was not under the auspices of the federal government. Their unauthorized teacher examination competed with the federally sponsored ones. As one historian noted, "It was purely a Chickasaw affair with Chickasaw licenses being granted."[59]

With their school funds cut off, the Chickasaws ran out of money to pay their teachers and contractors. Benedict smugly reported that as they "had not sufficient funds to meet the current expenses, these schools are being now financially embarrassed."[60] Hence the Chickasaws faced a terrible dilemma and a mounting crisis, for they could not obtain funds to "pay any of the employees or teachers," who had to wait more than a year for a paycheck.[61] Several neighborhood schools closed after the unpaid teachers quit. In addition, the Chickasaws had no money to spend on the upkeep of the school buildings. Benedict condemned the Rock Academy as unsafe.[62]

Forced to compromise, Johnston drew up an agreement with Benedict and Secretary Hitchcock. Johnston conceded Benedict's right "to assist in the examination of teachers" and agreed to establish a board of examiners that would examine teaching applicants with regard to their qualifications.[63] Although Benedict wanted more control, Johnston argued that since the Chickasaws paid for their own schools, they should manage them. He further pointed out that Secretary Hitchcock controlled only one-fourth of the funds that the Chickasaws used to run their schools and should thus have no more than a quarter of the control over their management.[64]

In 1902 Secretary Hitchcock paid the Chickasaws their long overdue coal and asphalt royalties, in the expectation that they would soon open their doors to white students. When the Chickasaws refused to admit whites to their neighborhood schools, Secretary Hitchcock cut off their coal and asphalt royalties again.

In justifying the push to integrate Chickasaw schools, Benedict argued that Chickasaw children would learn to speak English more readily by being brought into contact with white children. Chickasaw parents countered by saying that "they did not want their children to associate with white children because the latter taught them how to swear."[65] The Chickasaws protested that white students had no right to their exclusive education funds. When Americans agitated for the opening of tribal schools to noncitizens, the Chickasaws defended their schools as their birthright, purchased with funds secured through the sale of their Mississippi homeland. The Chickasaws did not want their educational funds siphoned off by noncitizens. They watched warily as U.S. inspectors, superintendents, and supervisors tried to transfer their schools, built with Chickasaw funds, to the white residents of Indian Territory.

The Chickasaws realized that once white children entered their schools, white administrators would remake their schools to suit them. While the other members of the Five Tribes admitted white children into their schools for a fee, the Chickasaws "steadily refused" to grant admittance to non-Indians. Some Choctaws attended Chickasaw schools on a fee basis, but white and black students were excluded. In 1895 U.S. Indian agent Drew Wisdom falsely reported that there were no facilities in the Chickasaw Nation in which white children could "obtain even the ordinary rudiments of an English education."[66] According to the Chickasaw superintendent of education, Charles D. Carter, noncitizens were "permitted to build schoolhouses and have their own schools, which is being done in every neighborhood wherever there is a sufficient number to justify it."[67] The white schools were subscription schools, paid for by the children's families. In 1891 Baptists built, supported, and managed Dawes Academy in Berwyn for black students, and the United States established a school at Fort Arbuckle for freedpeople.[68] In 1899 the Chickasaw government passed a bill to provide for the expenses of Chickasaw children who attended white subscription schools instead of Chickasaw neighborhood schools (due to space limitations).

In 1904, when the federal government made appropriations for public schools in Indian Territory, Benedict refused to allot any of the $100,000 appropriation to Chickasaw schools because the Chickasaws continued to refuse to admit white students to their schools. Moreover, Chickasaw children had to pay tuition if they wanted to attend one of the sixty new public schools established in their nation out of congressional funds. Choctaw children whose parents resided in the Chickasaw Nation did not.[69]

While some whites sympathized with the Chickasaws, others believed that the United States was right to subsidize only white children's education. In their view, not only should the United States pay the expenses of white schools, Indians should be barred from them, as blacks were, on account of their racial inferiority. One reporter noted that whites "don't believe in allowing the redskins these privileges."[70] In the end, the white and Indian schools merged, but blacks remained segregated. Oklahoma's constitution defined Indians as part of the "dominant" race, while relegating Indians of partial African descent to separate schools in the Jim Crow state.[71]

The Chickasaws defiantly held onto their schools until statehood, at which point they lacked sufficient resources to operate them any longer. When the Chickasaw school system changed to American hands in 1906, the date of the Chickasaw government's termination, the numbers of Chickasaw students attending school dropped off dramatically. The Chickasaws showed their opposition to federal control over Bloomfield Academy by refusing to send their daughters there any longer. Whereas under tribal control the average attendance was one hundred students, under the first year of federal control the average attendance was only twenty-four students, and it dropped even further the next year.[72] In addition, many Chickasaws refused to send their children to state-controlled neighborhood schools. National secretary Martin Cheadle explained the Chickasaws' change in attitude:

> The people rather rebel at the Government taking the schools away from us. We had been running the schools successfully for a great many years, and had spent a great deal of money and graduated our children every year. We had a high curriculum and turned out finished pupils every year. But on account of the expense the Government thought it was too much, and undertook to take the schools away, and now under the new system, the people won't send their children. The schools are not running, but the expense goes on just the same.[73]

In the Chickasaws' view, whites were taking advantage of them and defrauding them of their limited school funds. Cheadle noted that under the federal government's control, Chickasaws "don't know how our money is spent." The Five Tribes' boarding schools and academies were more than half empty, yet the cost to the Indian nations was greater.[74] Charges against the federally run Indian schools included poor food, cold rooms, and inattention to the students' medical care.[75]

In 1907 a group of former Chickasaw legislators petitioned Congress either to abolish the Chickasaws' schools or to restore them to the supervision of their tribal officers. They maintained that the schools under the new system were "both extremely expensive and unsatisfactory and afford a very small percentage of the Chickasaw children educational advantages." Their memorial was tabled. There was no consideration of returning the schools to Chickasaw supervision, nor could they be abolished until the Indians' lands were taxable.[76]

Most Chickasaws resented the changes they saw. The Bureau of Indian Affairs replaced Chickasaw superintendents with those of their own appointment, reduced the school year from ten to nine months, and relocated primary schools to areas that were more convenient to white communities and less accessible to Indians. The new superintendents imposed a statewide standardized curriculum and textbooks.[77] In 1910 the Dawes Commission reported less than 50 percent attendance at the Chickasaw schools. The commission made several excuses for the poor showing of the schools under federal control, such as the students' dislike for the new curriculum and their parents' or guardians' neglect. But mainly the commission blamed Chickasaw officials for "trying to break down the schools with the hope of securing their discontinuance as soon as possible." Certainly the commission was biased in its assessment, for that very year Benedict was suspended for neglect of duty and "business relationships of questionable character with the Indians."[78]

For as long as possible, the Chickasaws resisted the federal government's intrusion into school matters. They struggled to maintain their own schools because they were the means of inculcating Chickasaw pride and maintaining Chickasaw language and culture. Furthermore, their schools provided income and jobs for Chickasaw professionals, who had fewer opportunities than whites to find nonmanual jobs. After a congressional act of 1906 provided for the coeducation of blacks, Indians, and whites in Indian Territory, U.S. district schools absorbed and replaced Chickasaw neighborhood tribal schools. Gradually, the academies closed, too. In 1916 a disgruntled Chickasaw student set fire to Collins Institute for boys, now under federal control.[79]

Bloomfield Academy burned down, too, but the Chickasaws rebuilt it at another location. In 1910, when Chickasaw Annie Ream Addington took over as its superintendent, Chickasaw opposition decreased and its attendance improved.[80] Johnston, who continued as governor until his death in 1939, staunchly defended its continued existence. Bloomfield Academy was the last Indian boarding school to close, in 1949.

Finally, Chickasaw students were largely integrated with the white student population. (In the new state of Oklahoma, blacks were segregated by Jim Crown legislation.) On Statehood Day, September 1907, Oklahoma schools held a parade in which they "put the Indian children in front." Some of the older children refused to join the march; one such child expressed anger at his little brother for "yelling for Statehood and giving up his land."[81]

The great experiment of the comprehensive Chickasaw academic program, which sought to provide educational opportunity for the young in order to sustain tribal culture, traditions, and language, had ended. In the long run, the U.S. government proved too strong and the Chicka-

saws too weak to retain their school autonomy and tribal authority. However, based on the fact that the Chickasaws held out longer in preserv-
ing their schools and other shreds of autonomy (for example, winning
Supreme Court cases to revisit Citizen Court cases and compensation
for lands given to freedpeople), we might conclude that the Chickasaw schools succeeded admirably in producing civic-minded, intelli-
gent citizens.

Epilogue

The End of Chickasaw Sovereignty

On various occasions in the nineteenth century, the Chickasaws contested non-Chickasaw claims to their national funds and lands. The results were mixed and often had unintended results. Once the Chickasaws had reestablished their self-government in 1856, they demanded the removal from their lands of the western Indians who had claims to the same territory, based on prior occupancy. The Chickasaw Nation was numerically weak and depended on U.S. troops to protect it from Comanches, Texans, and white intruders. Under treaty stipulations, the U.S. government was obligated to protect the Five Tribes from intrusion; however, it rarely intervened except to force the Indians to accept freedpeople, railroads, and other uninvited parties into their lands. U.S. inaction left the security of the Indian governments severely compromised.[1]

Another threat to Chickasaw sovereignty emerged from freedpeople's claims to Indian citizenship. The United States refused to expel former slaves from the Chickasaws' lands, even those who had no legitimate claims to freedperson status. After statehood (1907), Indians and blacks found very different positions in Oklahoma's racial order, and the Chickasaws' tough stance toward not adopting their freedpeople proved valuable (as they received payment for Chickasaw freedpeople's allotments).

The railroads brought more and more settlers into the area, who, in turn, became more and more invested in the enterprises and farms they secured on land rented from Chickasaw individuals. Since the Chickasaw Nation was the smallest in population with the most acreage available, it became a magnet for white and black settlers. The repeated attempts of Congress to detribalize the Chickasaw Nation aggravated stresses within the nation, and violence sometimes threatened to rent the nation apart during elections and during the Chickasaw militia's enforcement of the permit law. Because the Chickasaws wanted to hold onto the lands and rights that were rightfully theirs, the National Party became the predominant political force of the late nineteenth century, from 1874 to 1902.

Most Chickasaws resisted total cultural assimilation (even those participating in upward economic mobility in white society) because the social and economic advantages tied to their collective national identity outweighed the disadvantages. In many instances, individuals' livelihood depended on their access to common lands and annuities. Chickasaw leaders lobbied tirelessly to preserve the rights that were guaranteed to them in U.S. treaties.

In 1893 Congress established a permanent commission to pressure the Five Tribes to abandon their tribal governments, accept allotments of land in severalty, and become U.S. citizens. The Dawes Commission met significant resistance from Chickasaws of the National Party, who were determined to delay the denationalization of their people for as long as possible. Although bullied by commissioners, the Chickasaw people rejected the Atoka Agreement of 1897, which provided for their tribal dissolution. Over their objections, Congress passed the Curtis Act of 1898, which stripped the nation of meaningful sovereignty and demonstrated that the U.S. government had the power to impose its will on them.

In the end, Congress would not let the Chickasaw Nation determine who were the legitimate members of that nation, allowing many white claimants wrongfully to appeal to the Dawes Commission, territorial courts, and the Department of the Interior. All the while, the Chickasaws had to expend great sums of money to defend their rights and stave off efforts to dispossess them. They succeeded, with the passage of the Supplementary Agreement (1902), in creating a new court to reconsider hundreds of whites' suspicious claims to citizenship. One historian notes, "The Chickasaws demonstrated that if their government was going out of business it would not go quietly." The Citizenship Court afforded them "some limited autonomy while at the same time saving them a colossal sum of money."[2]

Even before Congress dissolved the Chickasaws' communal land base, it demanded that Chickasaw schools open their doors to non-Chickasaws. The Chickasaws were perhaps the best educated of the Five Tribes, investing the most money per student in their education system. The Chickasaws resisted total assimilation by attempting to retain control over their schools. Schools comprised a large part of the Chickasaws' economic well-being, and they were also a training ground for future tribal and community leaders. They provided a civic education that blended aspects of Indian and white cultures and instilled ethnic pride in Chickasaw youth. However, when the Chickasaws objected to the federal takeover of their schools, they lost access to their own royalty funds as well as to federal appropriations in the territory for public education. In 1901 all Indians of the territory became citizens, and with Oklahoma statehood in 1907, Indian Territory itself disappeared.

The Chickasaws' situation had some particulars that were uncharacteristic of most of the other members of the Five Tribes. For example, they held their land in trust with the Choctaws, who had to be a party to any contract with the federal government or a corporation involving land use or sale. After the Chickasaw government reestablished its independence from the Choctaw Nation, the two tribes still owned their lands in common. This anomalous situation helped the Chickasaws defeat Choctaw proposals that they regarded as inimical to their interests. These included Choctaw agreements to allot lands to freedpeople and grant railroad rights-of-way; the Chickasaws also successfully challenged thousands of whites' fraudulent legal claims to citizenship on the basis that they had not filed with both nations.

From 1907 to 1971 U.S. presidents appointed a Chickasaw governor to handle administrative matters. Douglas Johnston served for life and became involved with many unresolved land questions. The Chickasaw governors have been the bulwarks against the total disappearance of the tribe. Under the oversight of the Bureau of Indian Affairs, in 1971 the Chickasaws were authorized to elect their own governor. Since then, the Chickasaws have made a concerted effort to rebuild their nation. They reconstituted their tribal legislature in 1975 and adopted a constitution in 1979.[3]

In the twenty-first century the Chickasaws are a federally recognized tribe with a number of member benefits, such as health care services and scholarships. They have maintained their tribal identity, a measure of autonomy, and important cultural attributes. Their museum, newspapers, historical journals, cultural preservation projects, and publishing press have reinvigorated their celebration of their tribal heritage.

Notes

Introduction

1. James R. Atkinson, *Splendid Land, Splendid People: The Chickasaw Indians to Removal* (Tuscaloosa: University of Alabama Press, 2004).

2. Frederick Hoxie, "Ethnohistory for a Tribal World," *Ethnohistory* 14 (Fall 1997): 610.

3. United States, House Committee on Territories, *Granting Statehood to Oklahoma and Revising Boundary with Chickasaw Indian Lands*, 1893–94, 53rd Cong., 2nd sess., Bill 53, H.R. 4951.

4. Andrew Denson, *Demanding the Cherokee Nation: Indian Autonomy and American Culture, 1830–1900*, Indians of the Southeast (Lincoln: University of Nebraska Press, 2004), 6.

5. United States, House Committee on Territories, *Granting Statehood to Oklahoma*.

6. Alexandra Harmon, "American Indians and Land Monopolies in the Gilded Age," *Journal of American History* 90 (June 2003): 115; W. David Baird, "Are There 'Real' Indians in Oklahoma? Historical Perceptions of the Five Civilized Tribes," *Chronicles of Oklahoma* 68, no. 1 (1990): 4–23.

7. Editorial, *Purcell Register*, January 19, 1893, 1.

Chapter 1

1. "Union of the Choctaw and Chickasaws," *Arkansas Gazette*, May 11, 1830.

2. Villebeuvre to Carondelet, January 16, 1793, and Villebeuvre to Carondelet, February 4, 1793, in D. C. Corbitt and Roberta Corbitt, eds., "Papers from the Spanish Archives relating to Tennessee and the Old Southwest, 1783–1800," *East Tennessee Historical Society Publications* 29 (1957): 145, 148.

3. Charles Joseph Kappler and United States, *Indian Treaties, 1778–1883* (New York: Interland, 1972).

4. Chickasaw Chiefs to Jackson, May 28, 1831, Office of Indian Affairs, Chickasaw Agency, Letters Received, 1824–80, Record Group 75, microfilm 234, roll 136, National Archives and Records Administration, Washington, D.C.

5. Mary Elizabeth Young, *Redskins, Ruffleshirts and Rednecks: Indian Allotments in Alabama and Mississippi, 1830–1860*, Civilization of the American Indian (Norman: University of Oklahoma Press, 1961).

6. Horatio B. Cushman, *History of the Choctaw, Chickasaw, and Natchez Indians* (New York: Russell & Russell, 1972), 48.

7. Commissioners John Eaton and John Coffee to Secretary of War Cass, December 11, 1821, in United States, *Correspondence on the Subject of the Emigration of the Indians*, 23rd Cong., 1st sess., S. Doc. 512.

8. Ethan Allen Hitchcock, *A Traveler in Indian Territory: The Journal of Ethan Allen Hitchcock, Late Major-General in the United States Army*, ed. Grant Foreman (Cedar Rapids, Iowa: Torch, 1987), 200.

9. W. David Baird, *Peter Pitchlynn: Chief of the Choctaws*, Civilization of the American Indian 116 (Norman: University of Oklahoma, 1972), 8.

10. Ibid., 46.

11. John Pitchlynn to Peter Pitchlynn, September 13, 1834, Peter Pitchlynn Collection, box 1, folder 42, Thomas Gilcrease Institute of American History and Art, Tulsa, Okla.

12. Christopher C. Dean, *Letters on the Chickasaw and Osage Missions*, Missionary Series, Osage Mission, 9 (Boston: Massachusetts Sabbath School Society, 1833).

13. John Pitchlynn to Peter Pitchlynn, September 13, 1834.

14. Reynolds to Cass, December 9, 1832, Grant Foreman Collection, box 1, Thomas Gilcrease Institute of American History and Art, Tulsa, Okla.

15. John Pitchlynn to Peter Pitchlynn, January 30, 1835, Peter Pitchlynn Collection, box 1, folder 35.

16. John Pitchlynn to Peter Pitchlynn, January 10, 1835, Peter Pitchlynn Collection, box 1, folder 45.

17. Ibid.

18. William Armstrong, Choctaw Agent, to General Council of the Choctaw Nation, October 3, 1836, Grant Foreman Collection, box 1, folder 52.

19. John Eaton to Commissioner John Coffee, May 17, 1831, in *Correspondence on the Subject of the Emigration of the Indians*.

20. Memorial of the Chickasaws to President Andrew Jackson, Septem-

ber 1836, in Gaston L. Litton, ed., "Notes and Documents: The Negotiations Leading to the Chickasaw-Choctaw Agreement, January 17, 1837," *Chronicles of Oklahoma* 17, no. 4 (1939): 418.

21. Ibid.; "Union of the Choctaw and Chickasaw Indians," *Arkansas State Gazette,* February 14, 1837.

22. Chickasaw Delegation to Chiefs, Captains, and Warriors of the Choctaw Nation, January 11, 1837, in Litton, "Notes," 420.

23. Arrell Morgan Gibson, *The Chickasaws,* Civilization of the American Indian 109 (Norman: University of Oklahoma Press, 1971), 242.

24. Hitchcock, *Journal,* 173, 183.

25. Monte Ross Lewis, "Chickasaw Removal: Betrayal of the Beloved Warriors, 1794–1844" (Ph.D. diss., North Texas State University, 1981), 161.

26. Kingsbury to Harris, August 8, 1837, Office of Indian Affairs, Chickasaw Agency, Letters Received, 1837–38, microfilm 234, roll 143, National Archives, Washington, D.C.

27. Carolyn Thomas Foreman, "The Armstrongs of Indian Territory," *Chronicles of Oklahoma* 30, no. 4 (1952): 430.

28. "Report of the Commissioner of Indian Affairs," in United States, *Message from the President of the United States to the Two Houses of Congress, 1844,* 28th Cong., 2nd sess., H. Exec. Doc. 2, 299–502 (Washington, D.C.: Blair and Rives, 1844).

29. Hitchcock, *Journal,* 187.

30. Ibid.

31. Wendy St. Jean, "After Removal: Class and Ethnic Divisions in the Chickasaw Nation," *Journal of Chickasaw History* 5, no. 2 (1999): 7–20; Michael F. Doran, "Population Statistics of Nineteenth Century Indian Territory," *Chronicles of Oklahoma* 53, no. 4 (1975–76): 509.

32. Hitchcock, *Journal,* 187.

33. Ibid.

34. Richard Green, "Malcolm McGee Chickasaw Interpreter," *Journal of Chickasaw History* 4, no. 4 (1998): 8.

35. Chickasaw County Courts, July 1869, CKN 16, Chickasaw microfilm publications, Indian Archives Collection, Supreme Court, District Court, Attorney General Reports, 1858–1907. Archives and Manuscript Division, Oklahoma Historical Society.

36. Chickasaw Nation, *Constitution, Laws, and Treaties of the Chickasaws by Authority* (1860; repr., Wilmington, Del.: Scholarly Resources, 1975), 88.

37. Cushman, *History of the Choctaw, Chickasaw and Natchez Indians,* 518.

38. Upshaw to Indian Commissioner, August 16, 1845, Office of Indian Affairs, Chickasaw Agency, Letters Received, 1853–55, microfilm 234, roll 141, frame 114.

39. Hitchcock, *Journal,* 172.

40. "Report of the Commissioner of Indian Affairs," in United States, *Message from the President of the United States to the Two Houses of Congress, 1843,* 28th Cong., 1st sess., H. Exec. Doc. 2, 269–468 (Washington, D.C.: Blair and Rives, 1843).

41. Indian Territory and James E. Reynolds, *Letter to the President of the United States from Delegates Representing the Indian Territory: Protesting against the Decision of the District Court for the Western District of Arkansas in the Case of Ex Parte James E. Reynolds* (Washington, D.C., 1878).

42. Greg O'Brien, *Choctaws in a Revolutionary Age, 1750–1830* (Lincoln: University of Nebraska Press, 2002), 111,

43. St. Jean, "After Removal"; Doran, "Population Statistics," 509.

44. Chickasaw Agent A. Smith to George Manypenny, October 9, 1853, Office of Indian Affairs, Chickasaw Agency, Letters Received, 1853–55, microfilm 234, roll 141, frame 34.

45. Baird, *Peter Pitchlynn,* 67, 96.

46. "Report of the Commissioner of Indian Affairs," in United States, *Annual Message of the President and Report of the Secretary of the Interior, 1855,* 34th Cong., 1st sess., S. Exec. Doc. 1, pt. 1, 321–576 (Washington, D.C.: Government Printing Office, 1855).

47. Cooper to Thomas Drew, September 3, 1853, Office of Indian Affairs, Chickasaw Agency, Letters Received, 1853–55, microfilm 234, roll 141, frame 167.

48. Claiborne to Harris, November 3, 1837, Office of Indian Affairs, Chickasaw Agency, Letters Received, 1853–55, microfilm 234, roll 141, frame 137.

49. Jacob Folsom to Peter Pitchlynn, October 20, 1841, Peter Pitchlynn Collection, box 1, folder 69; Grant Foreman, *The Five Civilized Tribes* (Norman: University of Oklahoma Press, 1934), 107.

50. Robert M. Jones to Peter Pitchlynn, July 13, 1848, Peter Pitchlynn Collection, box 2, folder 5.

51. "Overland Mail Expedition," *New York Herald,* March 15, 1858, 8.

52. James Allen to Wilson, February 9, 1855, American Indian Correspondence, Presbyterian Mission Records, microfilm C-19, box 11, reel 3, Western History Collection, University of Oklahoma Library, Norman, Okla.

53. United States, *Annual Report of the Commissioner of Indian Affairs to*

the Secretary of the Interior for 1843 (Washington, D.C.: Government Printing Office, 1844), 419–20.

54. Chickasaw Memorial to Choctaw National Council, October 19, 1852, Office of Indian Affairs, Choctaw Agency, microfilm 234, roll 173, frame 192, National Archives, Washington, D.C.

55. Juanita J. Keel Tate, *Edmund Pickens: First Elected Chickasaw Chief, His Life and Times* (Ada, Okla.: Chickasaw Press, 2008), 71.

56. Chickasaw Agent A. M. M. Upshaw to Commissioner Medill, September 10, 1846, Office of Indian Affairs, Chickasaw Agency, Letters Received, 1844–49, microfilm 234, roll 139.

57. Chickasaw Agent A. M. M. Upshaw to Commissioner Medill, April 25, 1848, Office of Indian Affairs, Chickasaw Agency, Letters Received, 1844–49, microfilm 234, roll 139; Duane Champagne, *Social Order and Political Change: Constitutional Governments among the Cherokee, the Choctaw, the Chickasaw, and the Creek* (Stanford, Calif: Stanford University Press, 1992), 193.

58. William M. Guy to James Gamble, July 15, 1857, Papers of Governor William Guy, Western History Collection, University of Oklahoma Library, Norman, Okla.

59. Ibid.

60. Chickasaw Delegates to George Manypenny, April 14, 1855, Chickasaw Agency, Letters Received, 1853–55, microfilm 234, roll 141.

61. Ibid.

62. Chickasaw Agent A. Smith to George Manypenny, October 9, 1853, Office of Indian Affairs, Chickasaw Agency, Letters Received, 1853–55, microfilm 234, roll 141, frame 34.

63. Charles M. Hudson, *The Southeastern Indians* (Knoxville: University of Tennessee Press, 1976), 276.

64. Agent Smith to George Manypenny, October 9, 1853.

65. Thomas J. Pitchlynn to Peter Pitchlynn, December 22, 1852, Peter Pitchlynn Collection, box 2.

66. Douglas Cooper to Manypenny, April 16, 1855, memoranda of conversations with Chickasaw and Choctaw delegates, Office of Indian Affairs, Choctaw Agency, 1855–56, microfilm 234, roll 174.

67. J. Wall to Peter Pitchlynn, November 11, 1850, Peter Pitchlynn Collection, box 2, folder 17.

68. Thomas J. Pitchlynn to Peter Pitchlynn, December 22, 1852, Peter Pitchlynn Collection, box 2.

69. Choctaw Delegation to Manypenny, Washington, May 30, 1854, Office of Indian Affairs, Choctaw Agency, 1855–56, microfilm 234, roll 174.

70. Mary Young, "Conflict Resolution on the Indian Frontier," *Journal of the Early Republic* 16 (Spring 1996): 1.

71. Chickasaw Agent A. Smith to George Manypenny, in United States, *Annual Report of the Commissioner of Indian Affairs to the Secretary of the Interior for the Year 1855* (Washington, D.C.: Government Printing Office, 1856).

72. For a detailed description of the Treaty of 1855, see Muriel H. Wright, "Brief Outline of the Choctaw and Chickasaw Nations in Indian Territory, 1820 to 1860," *Chronicles of Oklahoma* 7, no. 4 (1929): 388–418.

73. Ibid.

Chapter 2

1. Levi Colbert to Andrew Jackson, February 23, 1832, Office of Indian Affairs, Chickasaw Agency, Letters Received, 1824–81, Record Group 75, microfilm 234, roll 136, frame 261, National Archives and Records Administration, Washington, D.C.

2. Monte Ross Lewis, "Chickasaw Removal: Betrayal of the Beloved Warriors, 1794–1844" (Ph.D. diss., North Texas State University, 1981), 61.

3. United States, *American State Papers: Indian Affairs,* vol. 2 (Washington, D.C.: Gales & Seaton, 1832): 721–23; Journal of 1826, Office of Indian Affairs, Chickasaw Agency, Letters Received, 1824–81, microfilm 234, roll 135.

4. United States, *American State Papers,* 723.

5. Congressional serial set, 22nd Cong., 1st sess., 1831–32, H.R. Doc. 488, 17–19.

6. David LaVere, *Contrary Neighbors: Southern Plains and Removed Indians in Indian Territory* (Norman: University of Oklahoma Press, 2000), 80; Armstrong to Crawford, May 16, 1839, Office of Indian Affairs, Chickasaw Agency, Letters Received, 1824–81, microfilm 234, roll 137, frame 491.

7. Grant Foreman, ed., "The Journal of the Proceedings at our First Treaty with the Wild Indians, 1835," *Chronicles of Oklahoma* 14, no. 4 (1936): 402.

8. LaVere, *Contrary Neighbors,* 81.

9. Lewis, "Chickasaw Removal," 145.

10. Upshaw to Armstrong, August 25, 1842, Office of Indian Affairs, Chickasaw Agency, Letters Received, 1824–81, microfilm 234, roll 138, frame 343.

11. LaVere, *Contrary Neighbors,* 55–56.

12. Lewis, "Chickasaw Removal," 161; Kingsbury to Harris, August 8, 1837, Office of Indian Affairs, Chickasaw Agency, Letters Received, 1837–38, microfilm 234, roll 143.

13. Collins to Harris, September 2, 1837, Miscellaneous Chickasaw Records, February 4, 1832–August 25, 1847, Record Group 75, National Archives and Records Administration, Washington, D.C.; Lewis, "Chickasaw Removal," 170.

14. Kingsbury to Armstrong, May 25, 1839, Office of Indian Affairs, Chickasaw Agency, Letters Received, 1824–81, microfilm 234, roll 137, frames 498–506.

15. William Paul, "Between Two Streams: Smith Paul Family," *Washita Valley* (Spring 1980): 4.

16. James M. Day and Dorman H. Winfrey, eds., *The Indian Papers of Texas and the Southwest, 1825–1916* (Austin: Pemberton, 1969), 1:122–23.

17. Randolph Barnes Marcy, *Thirty Years of Army Life on the Border* (Philadelphia: Lippincott, 1963), 171.

18. Kingsbury to Armstrong, May 19, 1839, Office of Indian Affairs, Chickasaw Agency, Letters Received, 1824–81, microfilm 234, roll 137, frame 502.

19. Ibid.

20. Ibid., frame 503.

21. Kingsbury to Armstrong, May 25, 1839, Office of Indian Affairs, Chickasaw Agency, Letters Received, 1824–81, microfilm 234, roll 137, frame 498.

22. Records of the Chickasaw Delegation, April 29, 1851, CKN 30, vol. 53, Chickasaw National Records, 1837–55, Indian Archives Division, 1877–81; CKN 16, Chickasaw Supreme Court, District Court, Attorney Generals' Reports and Other Records, 1858–1907, Chickasaw National Records, Indian Archives Division, 1977–81; CKN 30, Federal and Foreign Relations, 1848–65, all in Oklahoma Historical Society.

23. Editorial, *Choctaw Intelligencer,* June 11, 1851.

24. Lea to Harper, May 10, 1851, microfilm CKN 30, vol. 53, Chickasaw National Records, Indian Archives Division, 1977–81; CKN 10, vols. 53, 60, 54, Chickasaw County Court Records, Pickens and Wichita Counties, 1849–81, Oklahoma Historical Society.

25. Agreement between the Chickasaws and Delawares, June 16, 1853, microfilm CKN 10, vol. 53, Chickasaw National Records.

26. Records of the Chickasaw Delegation, April 29, 1851.

27. Ethan Allen Hitchcock, *A Traveler in Indian Territory: The Journal of*

Ethan Allen Hitchcock, Late Major-General in the United States Army, ed. Grant Foreman (Cedar Rapids, Iowa: Torch, 1987), 258.

28. Major James O'Neal of the Texas Militia to the Chickasaws, July 6, 1842, Office of Indian Affairs, Chickasaw Agency, Letters Received, microfilm 234, roll 138, frame 1007.

29. Records of the Chickasaw Delegation, April 29, 1851.

30. Monte Lewis, "The Chickasaw on the Texas Frontier," *West Texas Historical Association Year Book* 58 (1982): 137; Hitchcock, *Journal,* 256–57; Day and Winfrey, *Indian Papers of Texas and the Southwest,* 2:128–43.

31. Day and Winfrey, *Indian Papers of Texas and the Southwest,* 1:132–34.

32. Ibid., 1:127.

33. "Indian Difficulties on the Frontier," *New York Herald,* May 25, 1848, 4.

34. Hitchcock, *Journal,* 258.

35. Ibid., 185.

36. Day and Winfrey, *Indian Papers of Texas and the Southwest,* 1:50.

37. Drew to Manypenny, January 24, 1854, Office of Indian Affairs, Chickasaw Agency, Letters Received, 1853–55, microfilm 234, roll 141, frame 148.

38. Neighbors to Medill, January 6, 1847. P-I 1087, Pamphlets in American History, American Antiquarian Society, Worcester, Mass.

39. "Legal Proceedings," *Farmer's Cabinet,* March 8, 1855, 2.

40. Report of the U.S. Indian Inspector, November 9, 1881, Records of the Indian Territory Division, Textual Records: Letters Sent, 1898–1907, with Index, 1898–99; Letters Received, 1898–1907, with Registers and Indexes, Special Files, 1898–1907; Final Membership Rolls of the Five Civilized Tribes, 1899–1914; Reports of Inspections of the Field Jurisdictions of the Office of Indian Affairs, 1873–1900, Records of the Office of the Secretary of the Interior, Record Group 48, microfilm 1070, roll 55, National Archives, College Park, Md.

41. Josiah Gregg, *Commerce of the Prairies,* ed. Max Moorhead, American Exploration and Travel (Norman: University of Oklahoma Press, 1954), 2:266.

42. Randolph Barnes Marcy, *Marcy and the Gold Seekers: The Journal of Captain R. B. Marcy, with an Account of the Gold Rush over the Southern Route,* ed. Grant Foreman (Norman: University of Oklahoma Press, 1939), 135.

43. George Washington to Cyrus Harris, January 8, 1868, in United States, *Outrages Committed by Indians on Western and Southwestern Frontiers,* 41st Cong., 2nd sess., H.R. Misc. Doc. 139, 3.

44. Chickasaw Nation, *Constitution, Laws, and Treaties of the Chickasaws by Authority* (1860; repr., Wilmington, Del.: Scholarly Resources, 1975), 163.

45. Wendy St. Jean, "After Removal: Class and Ethnic Divisions in the Chickasaw Nation," *Journal of Chickasaw History* 5, no. 2 (1999): 7–20.

46. Gregg, *Commerce of the Prairies,* 2:258, 401.

47. Hitchcock, *Journal,* 185.

48. U.S. Department of the Interior, *Annual Report of the Commissioner of Indian Affairs for the Year 1847,* 30th Cong., 1st sess. (Washington, D.C.: Wendell & Benthuysen, 1848); T. Lindsay Baker and Julie P. Baker, eds., *The WPA Oklahoma Slave Narratives* (Norman: University of Oklahoma Press, 1996), 324.

49. William Parker, *Through Unexplored Texas* (Austin: Texas State Historical Association, 1984), 29.

50. Hitchcock, *Journal,* 66; Parker, *Through Unexplored Texas,* 25.

51. "Keechi Raiders," *Mississippi Free Trader and Natchez Daily Gazette,* August 4, 1843.

52. Interview with John Criner, Indian-Pioneer History, vol. 2, Oklahoma Historical Society, Oklahoma City, Okla.

53. "Indian Appropriation Bill," *Galveston Daily News,* January 30, 1885.

54. David LaVere, ed., *Life among the Texas Indians: The WPA Narratives,* Elma Dill Russell Spencer Series in the West and Southwest 18 (College Station: Texas A & M University Press, 2006), 59.

55. Editorial, *Choctaw Intelligencer,* June 11, 1851.

56. Gary Clayton Anderson, *The Conquest of Texas: Ethnic Cleansing in the Promised Land, 1820–1875* (Norman: University of Oklahoma Press, 2005), 229.

57. "Comanches on the Rise," *Daily National Intelligencer,* October 7, 1858.

58. Douglas Cooper, "A Journal Kept by Douglas Cooper on an Expedition by a Company of Chickasaws in Quest of Comanche Indians," ed. Grant Foreman, *Chronicles of Oklahoma* 5, no. 4 (1927): 389–90.

59. "Message of Cyrus Harris," *Daily Morning News,* June 20, 1861.

60. Albert Rennie, "Pauls Valley Pioneer Is Visiting Here: Mrs. Sippia Hull Is Only Living First Resident of Pauls Valley," *Pauls Valley Democrat,* May 30, 1929.

61. Arrell Morgan Gibson and Victor E. Harlow, *The History of Oklahoma* (Norman: University of Oklahoma Press, 1984), 62.

62. LaVere, *Texas Indians,* 73.

63. United States, *Recent Raids and Outrages upon Citizens of Texas and in Chickasaw Nation by Bands of Kiowa and Comanche Indians,* 40th Cong., 2nd sess., 1867–68, S. Exec. Doc. 60, serial set 1317.

64. Cyrus Harris to Commissioner of Indian Affairs, January 23, 1868, in United States, *Outrages Committed by Indians on Western and Southwestern Frontiers;* Wilber Sturtevant Nye and William S. Soule, *Plains Indian Raiders: The Final Phases of Warfare from the Arkansas to the Red River* (Norman: University of Oklahoma Press, 1968), 113; I. G. Vane, clerk to Montford Johnson, Union Agency, March 16, 1882, Edward Bryant Johnson Papers, box 1, folder 1, Western History Collection, University of Oklahoma Library, Norman, Okla.

65. Gibson and Harlow, *History of Oklahoma,* 90.

66. LaVere, *Contrary Neighbors,* 37.

67. "Report of the Commissioner of Indian Affairs," in United States, *Report of the Secretary of the Interior, 1885,* 49th Cong., 1st sess., H. Exec. Doc. 1, pt. 5, vol. 2, 3–872 (Washington, D.C.: Government Printing Office, 1885).

68. Neil R. Johnson and C. Neil Kingsley, *The Chickasaw Rancher* (Boulder: University Press of Colorado, 2001).

69. John H. Moore, *The Cheyenne,* Peoples of America (Cambridge, Mass: Blackwell, 1996), 278.

70. Jon T. Kilpinen, "The Supreme Court's Role in Choctaw and Chickasaw Dispossession," *Geographical Review* 94, no. 4 (2004): 491–92.

71. Memorial to the Commissioner of Indian Affairs, 1865, Pamphlets in American History, I-989, 11, American Antiquarian Society.

Chapter 3

1. "Report of the Commissioner of Indian Affairs," in United States, *Annual Report of the Secretary of the Interior, 1865,* 39th Cong., 1st sess., H. Exec. Doc. 1, vol. 2, 169–772 (Washington, D.C.: Government Printing Office, 1866).

2. Jon T. Kilpinen, "The Supreme Court's Role in Choctaw and Chickasaw Dispossession," *Geographical Review* 94, no. 4 (2004): 493.

3. J. D. C. Atkins to Secretary of the Interior, May 8, 1888, in United States, *A Letter from the Commissioner of Indian Affairs Relative to the Freedmen in the Chickasaw Nation,* 50th Cong., 1st sess., S. Exec. Doc. 166, 2.

4. James H. Merrell, "The Racial Education of the Catawba Indians," *Journal of Southern History* 50, no. 3 (1984): 379.

5. Michael F. Doran, "Population Statistics of Nineteenth Century Indian Territory," *Chronicles of Oklahoma,* 53, no. 4 (1975–76): 501.

6. T. Lindsay Baker and Julie P. Baker, eds., *The WPA Oklahoma Slave Narratives* (Norman: University of Oklahoma Press, 1996), 246–47, 324–25.

7. Ethan Allen Hitchcock, *A Traveler in Indian Territory: The Journal of Ethan Allen Hitchcock, Late Major-General in the United States Army,* ed. Grant Foreman (Cedar Rapids, Iowa: Torch, 1987), 187.

8. Daniel F. Littlefield, *The Chickasaw Freedmen: A People without a Country,* Contributions in Afro-American and African Studies 54 (Westport, Conn: Greenwood, 1980), 12–15.

9. Chickasaw Nation, *Constitution, Laws, and Treaties of the Chickasaws by Authority* (1860; repr., Wilmington, Del.: Scholarly Resources, 1975), 115; Littlefield, *Chickasaw Freedmen,* 208.

10. Fay A. Yarbrough, *Race and the Cherokee Nation: Sovereignty in the Nineteenth Century* (Philadelphia: University of Pennsylvania Press, 2008); Baker and Baker, *WPA Oklahoma Slave Narratives,* 13, 62–63, 65–66, 70, 100, 102, 104, 105, 107, 162–63, 180, 196, 219–20, 227, 233, 238, 277, 301, 305–6, 314, 360, 398, 408, 420, 445, 468, 484, 490, 492, 495, 506.

11. Chickasaw Nation, *Constitution, Laws, and Treaties of the Chickasaws,* 115; Littlefield, *Chickasaw Freedmen,* 208.

12. *Chickasaw Constitution of 1856,* General Files, 1854–56, D 304, National Archives and Records Administration, Washington, D.C.

13. Doran, "Population Statistics," 515.

14. Chickasaw Nation, *Constitution, Laws, and Treaties of the Chickasaws,* 79, 81, 96, 111; Littlefield, *Chickasaw Freedmen,* 13.

15. Harry Warren, "Some Chickasaw Chiefs and Prominent Men," *Publications of Mississippi Historical Society* 8 (1904): 567.

16. Colbert's address to the legislature is reprinted in Annie H. Abel, *The American Indian and the End of the Confederacy, 1863–1866* (Lincoln: University of Nebraska Press, 1993), 286.

17. John Sanborn to James Harlan, January 5, 1866, in "Report of the Commissioner of Indian Affairs," in United States, *Annual Report of the Secretary of the Interior, 1866,* 39th Cong., 2nd sess., H. Exec. Doc. 1, vol. 2, 1–362 (Washington, D.C.: Government Printing Office, 1867).

18. Editorial, *Bangor Daily Whig and Courier,* February 27, 1892.

19. "Bow and Arrows," *Kansas City Star,* September 17, 1906, 7.

20. "Chickasaw Freedmen," *St. Louis Globe-Democrat,* November 12, 1877, 4.

21. G. T. Olmstead to Parker, September 21, 1869, in United States, *Annual Report of the Commissioner of Indian Affairs to the Secretary of the Interior for the Year 1869* (Washington, D.C.: Government Printing Office, 1870), 408; Thomas F. Andrews, "Freedmen in Indian Territory: A Post Civil War Dilemma," *Journal of the West* 4, no. 3 (1965), 369.

22. United States, *Memorial of a Committee on Behalf of the Colored People of the Choctaw and Chickasaw Tribes of Indians Representing Their Grievances, and Praying the Adoption of Such Measures As Will Secure to Them Equal Rights and Privileges with White Citizens,* 41st Cong., 2nd sess., 1870, S. Misc. Doc. 106, 2 (Washington, D.C.: Government Printing Office, 1870).

23. Ibid.

24. "Message of B. F. Overton," *Vindicator,* September 20, 1876.

25. Chickasaw Nation, *Constitution, Laws, and Treaties of the Chickasaws,* 148; United States, *Report of Commission to the Five Civilized Tribes: Statement of the Chickasaw Freedmen Setting Forth Their Wrongs, Grievances, Claims, and Needs,* 53rd Cong., 3rd sess., 1894, S. Misc. Doc. 24, 109.

26. Chickasaw Memorial to the President of the United States, March 16, 1888, Records of the Office of the Secretary of the Interior, Special Files: Choctaw and Chickasaw and Cherokee Freedmen, Record Group 48, box 48, file 7773, National Archives and Records Administration, College Park, Md.; Murray R. Wickett, *Contested Territory: Whites, Native Americans, and African Americans in Oklahoma, 1865–1907* (Baton Rouge: Louisiana State University Press, 2000), 411; Walt Wilson, "Freedmen in Indian Territory during Reconstruction," *Chronicles of Oklahoma* 49, no. 2 (1971), 241.

27. Chickasaw Memorial to the President of the United States.

28. Wickett, *Contested Territory,* 268.

29. United States, *Report of Commission to the Five Civilized Tribes.*

30. Onis Gaines Jones, "Chickasaw Governors and Their Administrations to 1893" (Ph.D. diss., University of Oklahoma, 1935), 157.

31. Editorial, *Minco Minstrel,* June 22, 1894.

32. "Exodus to Oklahoma," *Atchison Daily Champion,* June 14, 1888; "Negroes Bound for Oklahoma," *Inter Ocean,* June 14, 1888.

33. Littlefield, *Chickasaw Freedmen,* 92.

34. Ibid.

35. Abel, *American Indian and the End of the Confederacy,* 298.

36. W. H. Twine to Secretary of the Interior C. N. Bliss, September 13, 1898, Records of the Office of the Secretary of the Interior, entry 705, Letters Received, box 2, file 396.

37. United States, *Report of the Select Committee to Investigate Matters Connected with Affairs in the Indian Territory with Hearings,* November 11, 1906–January 9, 1907, 59th Cong., 2nd sess., report no. 5013 (Washington, D.C.: Government Printing Office, 1907), 1:477; Melvin Cornish Collection, Western History Collection, box 20, folder 40, University of Oklahoma Library, Norman, Okla.

38. Interview with Emma Thompson Hampton, Indian-Pioneer Papers Collection, vol. 38, no. 12968, Western History Collection, University of Oklahoma Library, Norman, Okla.

39. Littlefield, *Chickasaw Freedmen,* 93.

40. Charles Cohee to Secretary of the Interior, October 29, 1902, Records of the Office of the Secretary of the Interior, no. 6848.

41. "Douglas Johnston's Annual Message," *Dallas Morning News,* September 5, 1907, 11.

42. Thomas Randolph to Secretary of the Interior, May 7, 1888, Records of the Office of the Secretary of the Interior, box 48, file 12988.

43. Ibid.; United States, *Executive Documents of the Senate of the United States,* 51st Cong., 1st sess. (Washington, D.C.: Government Printing Office, 1890), 50–54.

44. Barbara Krauthamer, "In Their 'Native Country': Freedpeople's Understandings of Culture and Citizenship in the Choctaw and Chickasaw Nations," in *Crossing Waters, Crossing Worlds,* ed. Tiya Miles and Sharon P. Holland (Durham, N.C.: Duke University Press, 2006), 116.

45. Delano to William A. Buckingham, in United States, *Relief of Certain Persons of African Descent Resident in Choctaw and Chickasaw Nation,* 43rd Cong., 1st sess., 1873–74, S. Misc. Doc. 118; Berlin Chapman, "Freedmen and the Oklahoma Lands," *Southwestern Social Science Quarterly,* September 1948, 154.

46. Douglas Johnston, *Argument on Behalf of the Chickasaw Nation against the Reopening of the Choctaw and Chickasaw Citizenship Rolls* (Washington, D.C.: Government Printing Office, 1910).

47. Wickett, *Contested Territory,* 207–8.

48. Johnston, *Argument on Behalf of the Chickasaw Nation.*

49. United States, *Citizenship in the Choctaw and Chickasaw Nations: Hearings before a Subcommittee on Indian Affairs,* House Report 15649 (Washington, D.C.: Government Printing Office, 1908).

50. Littlefield, *Chickasaw Freedmen,* 133; Wickett, *Contested Territory,* 124.

51. "What Douglas H. Johnston and Richard McLish Have Been Doing for the Past Twenty Years," 9, University of Tulsa Special Collections, Tulsa,

Okla.; Memorial to Congress, January 17, 1908, microfilm CKN 23, Chicka-
saw National Records, Oklahoma Historical Society, Oklahoma City, Okla;
Angie Debo, *And Still the Waters Run: The Betrayal of the Five Civilized Tribes*
(Princeton, N.J.: Princeton University Press, 1973), 41.

52. Wickett, *Contested Territory*, 27.

53. United States, *Survey of Conditions of the Indians in the United States:
Hearings before a Subcommittee of the Committee on Indian Affairs, United States
Senate*, 71st Cong., 2nd sess. (Washington, D.C.: Government Printing Office,
1931), 6860, 5362.

54. "Education in the New State," *Dallas Morning News*, November 6, 1907, 6.

Chapter 4

1. Kenneth H. Bobroff, "Retelling Allotment: Indian Property Rights and
the Myth of Common Ownership," *Vanderbilt Law Review* 54, no. 4 (2001).

2. David E. Wilkins, *American Indian Sovereignty and the U.S. Supreme
Court: The Masking of Justice* (Austin: University of Texas Press, 1997), 20.

3. Andrew Denson, *Demanding the Cherokee Nation: Indian Autonomy
and American Culture, 1830–1900*, Indians of the Southeast (Lincoln: University of Nebraska Press, 2004), 185.

4. Interview with George Nail, Indian-Pioneer History, vol. 66, no. 7453,
Oklahoma Historical Society, Oklahoma City,.

5. Interview with Jesse Maize, Indian-Pioneer Papers Collection, vol. 60,
no. 8444, Western History Collection, University of Oklahoma Library, Norman, Okla.

6. Interview with John T. Barr, Indian-Pioneer History, vol. 5, no. 9655.

7. Angie Debo, *And Still the Waters Run: The Betrayal of the Five Civilized
Tribes* (Princeton, N.J.: Princeton University Press, 1973), 59.

8. Parthena Louise James, "The White Threat in the Chickasaw Nation,"
Chronicles of Oklahoma 46, no. 1 (1968): 75.

9. James Gribble Hochtritt, "Rural Cherokees, Chickasaws, Choctaws,
Creeks, and Seminoles in Oklahoma during the Great Depression" (Ph.D.
diss., University of Oklahoma, 2000).

10. Agent Marston to Commissioner J. Q. Smith, March 20, 1877, in United
States, *Rights of Indians to Impose Taxes*, 45th Cong., 2nd sess., 1877–97, S.
Exec. Doc. 74, part 3, 22.

11. Overton's Message to the Chickasaw Nation, September 21, 1881, Re-

cords of the Office of the Secretary of the Interior, Record Group 48, microfilm 1070, roll 55, frame 268, National Archives and Records Administration, College Park, Md.

12. Annual Message of Gov. B. F. Overton to the Chickasaw Council, at Tishomingo City, September 7, 1880, *Pamphlets in American History: Indians,* I-679 (Glen Rock, N.J.: Microfilming Corp. of America, 1978).

13. Quoted in Arrell Morgan Gibson, *The Chickasaws,* Civilization of the American Indian 109 (Norman: University of Oklahoma Press, 1971), 287.

14. Loren N. Brown, "The Choctaw-Chickasaw Court Citizens," *Chronicles of Oklahoma* 16, no. 4 (1938): 8; interview with Zack Redford, Indian-Pioneer Papers Collection, vol. 74, no. 12467.

15. "Message of B. F. Overton," *Vindicator,* September 20, 1876.

16. Brown, "The Choctaw-Chickasaw Court Citizens," 3.

17. Debo, *And Still the Waters Run,* 16; "Overton's Resignation and Message to the Chickasaw Nation," *Sedalia Daily Democrat,* [?] 1881, 55.

18. Alexandra Harmon, "American Indians and Land Monopolies in the Gilded Age," *Journal of American History* 90, no. 1 (2003): 115.

19. Interview with Nannie Barcus, Indian-Pioneer Papers Collection, vol. 5, no. 13223.

20. Jim Skaggs, *Ranch and Range in Oklahoma* (Oklahoma City: Oklahoma Historical Society, 1978), 23.

21. Interview with George Harper, Indian-Pioneer Papers Collection, vol. 39, no. 7317.

22. "Disfranchised Chickasaws Alarmed," *St. Louis Republic,* November 4, 1889, 3; Harry F. O'Beirne, *Leaders and Leading Men of the Indian Territory, with Interesting Biographical Sketches of Choctaws and Chickasaws* (Chicago: American Publishers Association, 1891), iii; Mike Tower, *Outlaw Statesman: The Life and Times of Fred Tecumseh Waite* (Bloomington, Ind.: Authorhouse, 2007), 128.

23. Interview with Ida Sparks, Indian-Pioneer Papers Collection, vol. 86, no. 8788.

24. Grant Foreman, *Advancing the Frontier, 1830–1860* (Norman: University of Oklahoma Press, 1933), 285.

25. Interview with Oscar Lawrance, Indian-Pioneer History, vol. 52.

26. Harmon, "American Indians and Land Monopolies," 115.

27. Interview with Wyatt Chigley, Indian-Pioneer Papers Collection, vol. 17, no. 4640.

28. Interview with Chester Benn, Indian-Pioneer Papers Collection, vol. 7, no. 4430.

29. "News Item of Jonas Wolfe," *Purcell Register,* January 19, 1893.

30. Interview with George Lucas, Indian-Pioneer Papers Collection, vol. 56, no. 8659.

31. James Martin Yarborough, "The Transition of the Chickasaw Indians from an Organized Nation to a Part of a State" (master's thesis, Oklahoma Agricultural and Mechanical College, 1938), 137; "Message of Overton to the Legislature," *Star Vindicator,* September 29, 1876.

32. United States, *Rights of Indians to Impose Taxes.*

33. William Gerald McLoughlin, *After the Trail of Tears: The Cherokees' Struggle for Sovereignty, 1839–1880* (Chapel Hill: University of North Carolina Press, 1993), 349.

34. B. F. Grafton, *Argument of B. F. Grafton, Delivered January 24, 1879, before the Committee on Territories of the United States Senate in Opposition to Any Legislation That Will in Anywise Interfere with the Five Civilized Tribes Inhabiting the Indian Territory, or Annul Their Present Tribal Organizations, or Their Respective Legislatures or Judiciaries, or Their Rights, Laws, Privileges, or Customs, as Solemnly Guaranteed by Treaty Stipulations* (Washington, D.C.: Government Printing Office, 1879), 239.

35. Cole to President Grant, January 31, 1877, in United States, *Rights of Indians to Impose Taxes,* exhibit no. 11, 17.

36. Editorial, *Star Vindicator,* April 21, 1877; "Editorial on B. F. Overton," *Star Vindicator,* August 25, 1877.

37. Lem Reynolds to Secretary of the Interior Schurz, March 2, 1878, Records of the Office of the Secretary of the Interior, Record Group 48, microfilm 825, roll 32, frame 728.

38. Annual Message of Gov. B. F. Overton, 1880.

39. "Editorial on Letter of B. F. Overton," *Star Vindicator,* April 27, 1878.

40. McLoughlin, *After the Trail of Tears,* 349.

41. Ibid., 354.

42. "Fort Sill Country," *Dallas Morning News,* August 29, 1894, 6.

43. "Serious Hardships for Evicted Farmers," *St. Louis Republic,* July 30, 1891, 6; editorial, *Star Vindicator,* September 1, 1877.

44. "Attack upon Governor Overton," *Atoka Independent,* October 26, 1877.

45. Annual Message of Gov. B. F. Overton, 1880.

46. "White Intruders in the Indian Territory," *New York Times,* June 25, 1881, 2.

47. "Memorial of B. F. Overton," included in the Letter from the Secretary of the Interior, May 28, 1878, 45th Cong., 2nd sess., Exec. Doc. 87.

48. Lem Reynolds to Secretary of the Interior Schurz, March 2, 1878.

49. Interview with W. H. H. Keltner, Indian-Pioneer Papers Collection, vol. 50, no. 13199.

50. Interview with Luther Benjamin Haney, Indian-Pioneer Papers Collection, vol. 38, no. 9415.

51. U.S. Office of Indian Affairs, *Letter from the Secretary of the Interior, Transmitting a Report of the Commissary respecting Intruders into the Chickasaw and Choctaw Nations,* 51st Cong., 1st sess., 1889, S. Exec. Doc., vol. 12, no. 219, 74.

52. Interview with Oscar Lawrance, Indian-Pioneer History, vol. 52.

53. J. W. Rogers to Secretary of the Interior Schurz, January 9, 1878, Records of the Office of the Secretary of the Interior, Record Group 48, microfilm 825, roll 32, frame 499.

54. Peter Arthur to Secretary of the Interior Schurz, March 4, 1878, Records of the Office of the Secretary of the Interior, Record Group 48, microfilm 825, roll 32, frame 732.

55. "Message of B. F. Overton," *Atoka Independent,* September 14, 1877.

56. Judiciary Report no. 698, February 3, 1879, 45th Cong., 3rd sess.

57. Jeffery Burton, *Indian Territory and the United States, 1866–1906: Courts, Government, and the Movement for Oklahoma Statehood,* Legal History of North America 1 (Norman: University of Oklahoma Press, 1995), 184; National Indian Law Library and United States, *Landmark Indian Law Cases,* AALL Publications Series 65 (Buffalo, N.Y.: W. S. Hein, 2002), 447.

58. Letter of Overton, *Star Vindicator,* July 13, 1878; John Bartlett Meserve, "Governor Benjamin Franklin Overton and Governor Benjamin Crooks Burney," *Chronicles of Oklahoma* 16, no. 2 (1938): 226.

59. Duane Champagne, *Social Order and Political Change: Constitutional Governments among the Cherokee, the Choctaw, the Chickasaw, and the Creek* (Stanford, Calif: Stanford University Press, 1992), 224.

60. Governor Burney to Secretary of the Interior, October 18, 1880, Special Case 23: Chickasaw Nation: Cattle Laws, folder 8, National Archives and Records Administration, College Park, Md.

61. Ibid.

62. Meserve, "Governor Benjamin Franklin Overton," 228.

63. Interviews with Charles Darrow, and Paul Burney, Indian-Pioneer Papers Collection, vol. 23, no. 7397, and vol. 13, no. 12895.

64. Overton's Message to the Chickasaw Nation, September 21, 1881, Records of the Office of the Secretary of the Interior, Record Group 48, microfilm 1070, roll 55, frame 268.

65. Ibid.

66. Governor Burney to Secretary of the Interior, October 18, 1880.

67. "B. C. Burney Retired from Office," *Inter Ocean,* September 23, 1880, 4.

68. "Intruding on Indians," *Washington Post,* June 25, 1881, 1.

69. Interview with Ben Tillery, Indian-Pioneer Papers Collection, vol. 91, no. 4519.

70. Meserve, "Governor Benjamin Franklin Overton," 229.

71. United States, *Report on Indians Taxed and Indians Not Taxed in the United States at the Eleventh Census, 1890* (Washington, D.C.: Government Printing Office, 1894).

72. O'Beirne, *Leaders and Leading Men,* ix.

73. "Plan of Operation," *Rocky Mountain News,* June 12, 1891, 2.

74. "They Must Go," *Dallas Morning News,* May 17, 1891, 4.

75. Leona Stamps Barron, "The Penetration of Whites into the Chickasaw Nation, 1866–1907" (master's thesis, University of Oklahoma, 1939), 68.

76. Brown, "The Choctaw-Chickasaw Court Citizens," 16; Barron, "Penetration of Whites," 73.

77. "Hunting Up Intruders," *Dallas Morning News,* July 5, 1891, 10.

78. Editorial, *Purcell Register,* August 7, 1891.

79. "Hunting Up Intruders."

80. Interview with Zack Redford.

81. United States, *Report of the Commission Appointed to Negotiate with the Five Civilized Tribes of Indians, Known as the Dawes Commission,* 54th Cong., 1st sess., 1895, S. Doc. 12, 13–14.

82. Ibid.

83. Kent Carter, *The Dawes Commission and the Allotment of the Five Civilized Tribes, 1893–1914* (Orem, Utah: Ancestry.com, 1999), 182–84.

84. "Scandal in Interior Department Now: Dawes Commission Involved in Ugly Charges," *New York Times,* August 16, 1903.

85. Interview with Jake Williams, Indian-Pioneer History, vol. 88.

86. D. M. Vorhee to Carl Schurz, December 31, 1877, Records of the Office of the Secretary of the Interior, Record Group 48, microfilm 825, roll 32, frame 458.

87. Robert E. Bieder, "Scientific Attitudes toward Indian Mixed-Bloods," *Journal of Ethnic Studies* 8 (Summer 1980): 17–30.

88. Leonard A. Carlson, *Indians, Bureaucrats and the Land: The Dawes Act and the Decline of Indian Farming* (Westport, Conn.: Greenwood, 1981).

Chapter 5

1. Harry F. O'Beirne, *Leaders and Leading Men of the Indian Territory, with Interesting Biographical Sketches of Choctaws and Chickasaws* (Chicago: American Publishers Association, 1891), xi.

2. *Moore v. Carter,* October 1828, in Samuel H. Hempstead, ed. *Reports of Cases Argued and Determined in the United States Superior Court for the Territory of Arkansas, from 1820 to 1836* (Boston: Little, Brown, 1856).

3. Douglas Cooper to Indian Commissioner, August 20, 1859, "Report of the Commissioner of Indian Affairs," in United States, *Annual Message of the President and Report of the Secretary of the Interior, 1859*, 36th Cong., 1st sess., S. Exec. Doc. 2, vol. 1, 373–820 (Washington, D.C.: Government Printing Office, 1860).

4. O'Beirne, *Leaders and Leading Men,* 8.

5. "The Indian Problem," *Inter Ocean,* March 19, 1875, 2.

6. Interview with Thomas Randolph, Records of the Office of the Secretary of the Interior, Record Group 48, box 48, file 15841, National Archives and Records Administration, College Park, Md.

7. Erik March Zissu, *Blood Matters: The Five Civilized Tribes and the Search for Unity in the Twentieth Century* (New York: Routledge, 2001), 17.

8. John Bartlett Meserve, "Governor Cyrus Harris," *Chronicles of Oklahoma* 15, no. 4 (1937): 384; "Message of Cyrus Harris," *Vindicator,* September 14, 1872.

9. Meserve, "Governor Cyrus Harris," 384.

10. D. C. Gideon, *Indian Territory: Descriptive, Biographical, and Genealogical, Including the Landed Estates, County Seats, etc., etc., with a General History of the Territory* (New York: Lewis, 1901), 215–16.

11. Hart Maxcy Smith to mother, April 13, 1895, Hart Maxcy Smith Letters, Presbyterian Heritage Center, Montreat, N.C.

12. W. David Baird, *The Chickasaw People* (Phoenix: University of Arizona Press, 1976), 64.

13. James Martin Yarborough, "The Transition of the Chickasaw Indians from an Organized Nation to a Part of a State," (master's thesis, Oklahoma Agricultural and Mechanical College, 1938), 62; Chickasaw Nation, *Constitu-*

tion, Laws, and Treaties of the Chickasaws by Authority (1860; repr., Wilmington, Del.: Scholarly Resources, 1975), 143.

14. Murray R. Wickett, *Contested Territory: Whites, Native Americans, and African Americans in Oklahoma, 1865–1907* (Baton Rouge: Louisiana State University Press, 2000), 269.

15. Clara Sue Kidwell, *The Choctaws in Oklahoma: From Tribe to Nation, 1855–1970,* American Indian Law and Policy 2 (Norman: University of Oklahoma Press, 2007), 113.

16. Grand Jury Trial (1885), District Court Records, Chickasaw National Records, Oklahoma Historical Society, Oklahoma City, Okla.

17. "A Chickasaw Tragedy: Courting a Half-Breed Dangerous Business," *Inter Ocean,* June 2, 1876, 3.

18. Interview with Frank C. Wright, Indian-Pioneer History, vol. 100, Oklahoma Historical Society, Oklahoma City, Okla.

19. *C. C. Passmore vs. Choctaw and Chickasaw Nations,* Melvin Cornish Collection, Western History Collection, box 1, folder 14, University of Oklahoma Library, Norman, Okla.

20. Interview with Sara Burns, and interview with C. H. Eberle, Indian-Pioneer History, vols. 13, 27.

21. U.S. Joins Case, Choctaw and Chickasaw Citizenship Court, Cornish Collection, box 6, folder 19.

22. Interview with Robert Row, Indian-Pioneer History, vol. 79, no. 8701.

23. "Some Fresh and Interesting Information about the Indian Territory," *New York Times,* May 15, 1887, 6.

24. Interview with Frank C. Wright, Indian-Pioneer Papers Collection, vol. 100, Western History Collection, University of Oklahoma Library, Norman, Okla.

25. Interview with John Barr, Indian-Pioneer History, vol. 5, no. 9655.

26. Interview with Minnie Brown, Indian-Pioneer History, vol. 12, no. 7249.

27. Interview with Morris Brown, Indian-Pioneer History, vol. 12, no. 12380.

28. Interview with J. S. Bond, Indian-Pioneer History, vol. 9, no. 9510.

29. Interview with Hugh Beanor, Indian-Pioneer History, vol. 6, no. 8985.

30. Interview with J. H. Blackburn, Indian-Pioneer History, vol. 8, no. 4060.

31. Interview with Fannie Bell, Indian-Pioneer History, vol. 7, no. 6319.

32. Interview with Henry Tussey, Indian-Pioneer Papers, vol. 92.

33. U.S. Joins Case.

34. Wendy St. Jean, "'You Have the Land, I Have the Cattle': Intermarried

Whites and the Chickasaw Range Lands," *Chronicles of Oklahoma* 78 (Summer 2000): 182–95.

35. Velma Taliaferro, *Memoirs of a Chickasaw Squaw,* ed. Molly Levite Griffis (Norman, Oklahoma: Levite of Apache, 1987), 24.

36. Leona Stamps Barron, "The Penetration of Whites into the Chickasaw Nation, 1866–1907" (master's thesis, University of Oklahoma, 1939).

37. Editorial, *Purcell Register,* July 31, 1891.

38. Kidwell, *Choctaws in Oklahoma,* 108.

39. Ibid.

40. Editorial, *Atoka Independent,* May 19, 1888.

41. Memorial of the Chickasaw Nation, December 31, 1889, *Pamphlets in American History: Indians,* I-795 (Glen Rock, N.J.: Microfilming Corp. of America, 1978).

42. Editorial, *Fort Smith Elevator,* November 8, 1889.

43. Editorial, *Fort Smith Intelligencer,* September 5, 1890; "Chickasaw Legislature," *Dallas Morning News,* September 15, 1889, 3.

44. "Chickasaw Legislature," *Dallas Morning News,* September 8, 1889, 18; Court Records, Pickens County, 1864–93, roll CKN 11, Indian Archives Division, Oklahoma Historical Society, Oklahoma City, Okla.

45. "Disfranchised Chickasaws Alarmed," *St. Louis Republic,* November 4, 1889, 3; O'Beirne, *Leaders and Leading Men,* vi; "Chickasaw Election," *Dallas Morning News,* October 21, 1889, 6.

46. John Bartlett Meserve, "Governor William Leander Byrd," *Chronicles of Oklahoma* 12, no. 4 (1934): 438.

47. Editorial, *Fort Smith Intelligencer,* June 11, 1890.

48. "Chickasaw Legislature," *Dallas Morning News,* September 15, 1889, 3; Robert G. Hays, ed., *A Race at Bay:* New York Times *Editorials on "The Indian Problem," 1860–1900* (Carbondale: Southern Illinois University Press, 1997), 323.

49. Arrell Morgan Gibson, *The Chickasaws,* Civilization of the American Indian 109 (Norman: University of Oklahoma Press, 1971), 265.

50. Hays, *Race at Bay,* 345.

51. Kent Carter, "Deciding Who Can Be Cherokee," *Chronicles of Oklahoma* 69, no. 2 (1991): 179–80.

52. B. F. Grafton, *Argument of B. F. Grafton, Delivered January 24, 1879, before the Committee on Territories of the United States Senate in Opposition to Any Legislation That Will in Anywise Interfere with the Five Civilized Tribes Inhab-*

iting the Indian Territory, or Annul Their Present Tribal Organizations, or Their Respective Legislatures or Judiciaries, or Their Rights, Laws, Privileges, or Customs, as Solemnly Guaranteed by Treaty Stipulations (Washington, D.C.: Government Printing Office, 1879), 293.

53. Hays, *Race at Bay,* 344.

54. Editorial, *Indian Chieftain,* August 14, 1890, 2; editorial, *Boston Daily Globe,* August 31, 1890, 3.

55. "Chickasaw Election," *Dallas Morning News,* August 12, 1890, 1.

56. O'Beirne, *Leaders and Leading Men,* ix.

57. United States, *Report of the Commission Appointed to Negotiate with the Five Civilized Tribes of Indians, Known as the Dawes Commission,* 54th Cong., 1st sess., 1895, S.Doc. 12, 15, 59; editorial, *Purcell Register,* July 31, 1891.

58. Angie Debo, *And Still the Waters Run: The Betrayal of the Five Civilized Tribes* (Princeton, N.J.: Princeton University Press, 1973), 11.

59. Editorial, *Purcell Register,* July 31, 1891.

60. "Sam Paul's Test Case," *Dallas Morning News,* October 28, 1890, 8.

61. "Double Citizenship Sustained by the Department," *Cherokee Advocate,* February 25, 1891, 2.

62. "Report of Chickasaw Convention," *Cherokee Advocate,* January 21, 1891, 3.

63. Editorial, *Marlow Magnet,* November 2, 1893.

64. "President Arthur Pardons Sam Paul," *Cherokee Advocate,* March 14, 1884; "Chickasaw Election," *Indian Chieftain,* April 21, 1892.

65. Gideon, *Indian Territory,* 786–87.

66. "Sam Paul's Test Case"; "Father and Son Fight," *Inter Ocean,* December 11, 1890, 6.

67. "Squaw Men Will Act," *Kansas City Star,* June 20, 1894.

68. Loren N. Brown, "The Choctaw-Chickasaw Court Citizens," *Chronicles of Oklahoma* 16, no. 4 (1938): 429.

69. United States, *Report of the Commission to Negotiate with the Five Civilized Tribes, 1895,* 54th Cong. 1st sess., S. Doc. 182, vol. 7, 60 (Washington, D.C.: Government Printing Office), 1895.

70. Kent Carter, *The Dawes Commission and the Allotment of the Five Civilized Tribes, 1893–1914* (Orem, Utah: Ancestry.com, 1999), 183.

71. Michael W. Lovegrove, "Douglas Henry Johnston and the Chickasaw Nation, 1898–1939" (Ph.D. diss., University of Oklahoma, 1999).

72. U.S. Inspector Agent Hon. J. Geo. Wright to Sec. of Interior, September

29, 1899, Chickasaw Foreign Relations, microfilm CKN 24, doc. 7427, frame 299, Chickasaw National Records.

73. Ibid.

74. "Grafting on the Indians," *New York Times,* August 7, 1910.

75. Lovegrove, "Douglas Henry Johnston and the Chickasaw Nation," 109.

76. "What Douglas H. Johnston and Richard McLish Have Been Doing for the Past Twenty Years," 8, University of Tulsa Special Collections, Tulsa, Okla.

77. "Palmer Mosley Message," n.d., Papers of Governor Palmer Mosley, M-44, folder 9, Western History Collection, University of Oklahoma Library, Norman, Okla.

78. Brown, "The Choctaw-Chickasaw Court Citizens," 430–34.

79. "Grafting on the Indians."

Chapter 6

1. United States, *Survey of Conditions of the Indians in the United States: Hearings before a Subcommittee of the Committee on Indian Affairs, United States Senate,* 71st Cong., 2nd sess. (Washington, D.C.: Government Printing Office, 1931), 5356.

2. Balentine to Wilson, June 1, 1855, American Indian Correspondence, Presbyterian Mission Records, microfilm C-19, box 11, reel 3, Western History Collection, University of Oklahoma Library, Norman, Okla.

3. H. M. Greene to Wilson, February 21, 1855, American Indian Correspondence, microfilm C-19, box 11, reel 3; Thayer to Wilson, June 7, 1855, American Indian Correspondence, microfilm C-19, box 11, reel 3.

4. Eddy to Wilson, February 21, 1855, American Indian Correspondence, microfilm C-19, box 11, reel 3.

5. Walter Lowrie to Commissioner of Indian Affairs George W. Manypenny, January 1, 1857, reprinted in Muriel H. Wright, "Wapanucka Academy, Chickasaw Nation," *Chronicles of Oklahoma* 12, no. 4 (1934): 417.

6. Ibid., 419.

7. Amanda J. Cobb, *Listening to Our Grandmothers' Stories: The Bloomfield Academy for Chickasaw Females, 1852–1949* (Lincoln: University of Nebraska Press, 2000), 31.

8. Wright, "Wapanucka Academy," 420.

9. Josiah Gregg, *Commerce of the Prairies,* ed. Max Moorhead, American Exploration and Travel (Norman: University of Oklahoma Press, 1954), 2:261–62.

10. Caroline Davis, "Education of the Chickasaws, 1856–1907," *Chronicles of Oklahoma* 15, no. 4 (1937): 418.

11. Wright, "Wapanucka Academy," 420.

12. B. F. Grafton, *Argument of B. F. Grafton, Delivered January 24, 1879, before the Committee on Territories of the United States Senate in Opposition to Any Legislation That Will in Anywise Interfere with the Five Civilized Tribes Inhabiting the Indian Territory, or Annul Their Present Tribal Organizations, or Their Respective Legislatures or Judiciaries, or Their Rights, Laws, Privileges, or Customs, as Solemnly Guaranteed by Treaty Stipulations* (Washington, D.C.: Government Printing Office, 1879), 299.

13. Cobb, *Listening to Our Grandmothers' Stories,* 47.

14. Interview with Jim Cobb, Indian-Pioneer Papers Collection, vol. 18, no. 4033, Western History Collection, University of Oklahoma Library, Norman, Okla.

15. United States, *Annual Report of the United States Inspector for Indian Territory, Together with the Reports of the Superintendents of Schools in That Territory to the Secretary of the Interior for the Fiscal Year Ended June 30, 1900* (Washington, D.C.: Government Printing Office, 1900), 174.

16. Interview with Elizabeth Kemp Mead, Indian-Pioneer Papers Collection, vol. 61, no. 6218, Western History Collection, University of Oklahoma Library, Norman, Okla.

17. Interview with L. L. Sturdivant, Indian-Pioneer History, vol. 88, no. 10073, Oklahoma Historical Society, Oklahoma City, Okla.

18. Interview with Belle Chigley, Indian-Pioneer Papers Collection, vol. 17, no. 4930.

19. Davis, "Education of the Chickasaws," 419.

20. United States, *Annual Report of the United States Inspector for Indian Territory, Together with the Reports of the Superintendents of Schools in That Territory to the Secretary of the Interior for the Fiscal Year Ended June 30, 1899* (Washington, D.C.: Government Printing Office, 1899), 20.

21. Hart Maxcy Smith to mother, February 22, 1894, Hart Maxcy Smith Letters, Collections of the Historical Foundation of the Presbyterian and Reformed Churches, Presbyterian Heritage Center, Montreat, N.C. The author wishes to thank Bill Welge for sharing these letters.

22. Interview with Arthur Honnold, Indian-Pioneer Papers Collection, vol. 44, no. 7983.

23. Ibid.

24. United States, *Annual Report of the United States Inspector for Indian Territory, 1899,* 20.

25. Hart Maxcy Smith to father, December 7, 1895, Hart Maxcy Smith Letters.

26. Interview with Sam Mahardy, Indian-Pioneer Papers Collection, vol. 61, no. 6218.

27. "Message of Benjamin Franklin Overton," *Indian Journal,* September 20, 1883.

28. Hart Maxcy Smith to father, June 28, 1897, Hart Maxcy Smith Letters.

29. Davis, "Education of the Chickasaws," 429.

30. Hart Maxcy Smith, April 13, 1895, Hart Maxcy Smith Letters.

31. Hart Maxcy Smith to mother, January 24, 1896, Hart Maxcy Smith Letters.

32. Hart Maxcy Smith to mother, February 15, 1895, Hart Maxcy Smith Letters.

33. Hart Maxcy Smith to mother, November 28, 1895, Hart Maxcy Smith Letters.

34. Hart Maxcy Smith to father, May 25, 1897, Hart Maxcy Smith Letters.

35. "Message of July 19, 1897," Robert M. Harris Collection, box H-19, folder 13, Western History Collection, University of Oklahoma Library, Norman, Okla.

36. Interview with Elizabeth Kemp Mead.

37. Hart Maxcy Smith to father, October 18, 1896, Hart Maxcy Smith Letters.

38. "Chickasaw Nation Schools," *Dallas Morning News,* February 27, 1905, 2.

39. United States, *Annual Report of the Commissioner of Indian Affairs to the Secretary of the Interior for the Year 1891* (Washington, D.C.: Government Printing Office, 1891), 225; Chickasaw Nation, *Constitution, Laws, and Treaties of the Chickasaws by Authority* (1860; repr., Wilmington, Del.: Scholarly Resources, 1975), 286.

40. Superintendent John D. Benedict to Inspector J. W. Zevely, December 3, 1902, Record Group 48, entry 713, box 73, National Archives and Records Administration, Washington, D.C.

41. United States, *Annual Report of the Commissioner of Indian Affairs to the Secretary of the Interior for the Year 1899* (Washington, D.C.: Government Printing Office, 1899), 91–94.

42. Michael D. Green, "Chickasaw Nation to Statehood," in *Historical At-*

las of Oklahoma, ed. Charles Robert Goins, Danney Goble, and John Wesley Morris (Norman: University of Oklahoma Press, 2006), 104.

43. Cobb, *Listening to Our Grandmothers' Stories,* 72.

44. United States and William P. Blake, *Annual Reports of the Department of the Interior for the Fiscal Year Ended June 30, 1899,* Miscellaneous Reports, part 2 (Washington, D.C.: Government Printing Office, 1899), 23.

45. Cobb, *Listening to Our Grandmothers' Stories,* 57.

46. Interview with Elizabeth Kemp Mead.

47. Charles D. Carter, *Report of the Secretary of the Interior, Being Part of the Message and Documents Communicated to the Two Houses of Congress at the Beginning of the Second Session of the Fifty-fourth Congress* (Washington, D.C.: 1897), 2:157.

48. "Our Indians," *San Francisco Bulletin,* October 22, 1872, 2.

49. United States, *Annual Report of the United States Inspector for Indian Territory, 1899,* 21.

50. United States, *Annual Report of the Commissioner of Indian Affairs to the Secretary of the Interior for the Year 1900* (Washington, D.C.: Government Printing Office, 1900), 107; Joe C. Jackson, "Summer Normals in Indian Territory After 1898," *Chronicles of Oklahoma* 37, no. 3 (1959): 318.

51. Hart Maxcy Smith, June 4, 1894, Hart Maxcy Smith Letters; John Bartlett Meserve, "Governor William Leander Byrd," *Chronicles of Oklahoma* 12, no. 4 (1934): 438.

52. "Over the State," *Galveston Daily News,* September 22, 1881.

53. "Latest by Telegraph," *Daily Evening Bulletin,* May 10, 1881, 4; "Letter from Dallas," *Galveston Daily News,* May 15, 1881; "They Have an Organ," *St. Louis Globe-Democrat,* May 27, 1881, 4; "Dr. Saunders Buys an Interest in the *Herald,*" *Galveston Daily News,* May 27, 1881; "Arrival of Indian Governor and His Followers," *Galveston Daily News,* July 27, 1881; Marilyn Irvin Holt, *Indian Orphanages* (Lawrence: University Press of Kansas, 2001), 134.

54. "Indian School Funds," *Dallas Morning News,* September 2, 1903, 4.

55. "Schools in Territory," *Dallas Morning News,* October 27, 1900, 5; "Control over Choctaw Schools," *Dallas Morning News,* October 13, 1900, 7.

56. Douglas Johnston to Secretary of Interior, November 25, 1900, Record Group 48, entry 713, box 73, National Archives and Records Administration, Washington, D.C.

57. Ibid.; "An Explanation by Burton: No Chickasaw Duties since He Has Been Senator," *Kansas City Star,* August 24, 1905, 1.

58. Jackson, "Summer Normals," 318.

59. Joe C. Jackson, "Summer Normals in Indian Territory after 1898." *Chronicles of Oklahoma* 37, no. 3 (1959): 318n52.

60. United States, *Annual Report of the United States Inspector for Indian Territory, 1900,* 92.

61. United States, *Annual Report of the Commissioner of Indian Affairs to the Secretary of the Interior for the Year 1901* (Washington, D.C.: Government Printing Office, 1901), 221.

62. Wright, "Wapanucka Academy," 425; Davis, "Education of the Chickasaws," 444.

63. Davis, "Education of the Chickasaws," 441.

64. Superintendent John D. Benedict to Inspector J. W. Zevely, November 15, 1902, Record Group 48, entry 713, box 73, National Archives and Records Administration, Washington, D.C.

65. "The Chickasaw Indians: Missionary Moffatt Tells about Their Government and Their Habits," *Sun,* January 27, 1890.

66. United States, *Annual Report of the Commissioner of Indian Affairs to the Secretary of the Interior for the Year 1895* (Washington, D.C.: Government Printing Office, 1896), 162.

67. United States, *Annual Reports of the Department of the Interior for the Fiscal Year Ended June 30, 1897: Report of the Commissioner of Indian Affairs* (Washington, D.C.: Government Printing Office, 1897), 145.

68. United States, *Rights of Indians to Impose Taxes,* 45th Cong., 2nd sess., 1877–97, S. Exec. Doc. 74, exhibit no. 17, 24.

69. "Editorial on Chickasaw Schools," *South McAlester Capital,* October 20, 1904.

70. "Territory School Situation," *Dallas Morning News,* May 24, 1899, 8.

71. "Education in the New State," *Dallas Morning News,* November 6, 1907, 6.

72. Cobb, *Listening to Our Grandmothers' Stories,* 90, 112.

73. United States, *Report of the Select Committee to Investigate Matters Connected with Affairs in the Indian Territory with Hearings,* 59th Cong., 2nd sess., 1906, S. Doc. 5013, vol. 2, 927.

74. "Schools of the Chickasaws," *Dallas Morning News,* July 17, 1909, 3.

75. "Comforts Denied Indian Children," *Daily Oklahoman,* January 16, 1910, 3.

76. United States, *Memorial concerning Manner of Conducting Schools of the Chickasaw Nation,* 59th Cong., 2nd sess., 1906, S. Doc. 325.

77. "Indian Boarding Schools," *Dallas Morning News,* May 27, 1907, 9; Cobb, *Listening to Our Grandmothers' Stories,* 90, 112.

78. United States, "Report of the Commission to the Five Civilized Tribes," in *Report of the Secretary of the Interior* (Washington, D.C.: Government Printing Office, 1910), 444; "Indian Offices Abolished," *Philadelphia Inquirer,* February 20, 1910, 2.

79. "Pupil Fired School," *Kansas City Star,* May 10, 1916, 1; "Collins Institute Burns," *Dallas Morning News,* May 11, 1916, 5.

80. Cobb, *Listening to Our Grandmothers' Stories,* 88.

81. Interview with Alice Parker, Indian-Pioneer Papers Collection, vol. 69, no. 4020.

Epilogue

1. William Gerald McLoughlin, *After the Trail of Tears: The Cherokees' Struggle for Sovereignty, 1839–1880* (Chapel Hill: University of North Carolina Press, 1993), 354.

2. Michael W. Lovegrove, "Douglas Henry Johnston and the Chickasaw Nation, 1898–1939" (Ph.D. diss., University of Oklahoma, 1999), 86.

3. Jennifer Weldon Felmley, "'All Good Things Come from Below': The Origins of Effective Tribal Government" (Ph.D. diss., University of California, Berkeley, 2001).

Bibliography

Manuscript Collections

American Antiquarian Society, Worcester, Massachusetts (Full-text databases)
American Historical Newspapers
New York Times Archive
Nineteenth-Century Newspapers
Pamphlets in American History

Houghton Library, Harvard University, Cambridge, Massachusetts
American Board of Commissioners for Foreign Missions Papers, series 18.3.4

National Archives and Records Administration, College Park, Maryland
Records of the Office of the Secretary of the Interior, Record Group 48
Special Case 23: Chickasaw Nation: Cattle Laws
Special Files: Choctaw and Chickasaw and Cherokee Freedmen

National Archives and Records Administration, Washington, D.C.
Letters Sent by the Office of Indian Affairs, 1824–81
Office of Indian Affairs, Chickasaw Agency, Letters Received, 1824–80,
    Record Group 75
Office of Indian Affairs, Choctaw Agency

Newberry Library, Chicago
Choctaw Papers, Ayer Collection

Oklahoma Historical Society, Oklahoma City, Oklahoma
Chickasaw National Records

Choctaw National Records
Dawes Commission Records
Indian Archives Division
Indian-Pioneer History

Presbyterian Heritage Center, Montreat, North Carolina
Hart Maxcy Smith Letters

Thomas Gilcrease Institute of American History and Art, Tulsa, Oklahoma
Grant Foreman Collection
Peter Pitchlynn Collection

University of Oklahoma Library, Western History Collection,
Norman, Oklahoma
American Indian Correspondence, Presbyterian Mission Records, microfilm
C-19
Chickasaw Nation Collection
Choctaw Nation Collection
Edward Bryant Johnson Papers, 1882–1929
Gaston Litton Collection
Indian-Pioneer Papers Collection
Melvin Cornish Collection
Papers of Governor Benjamin Overton
Papers of Governor Douglas Johnston
Papers of Governor Jonas Wolf
Papers of Governor Palmer Mosley
Papers of Governor William Byrd
Papers of Governor William Guy
Robert M. Harris Collection

Published Sources

Abel, Annie H. *The American Indian and the End of the Confederacy, 1863–
   1866.* Lincoln: University of Nebraska Press, 1993.
Anderson, Gary Clayton. *The Conquest of Texas: Ethnic Cleansing in the Prom-
   ised Land, 1820–1875.* Norman: University of Oklahoma Press, 2005.
Atkinson, James R. *Splendid Land, Splendid People: The Chickasaw Indians to
   Removal.* Tuscaloosa: University of Alabama Press, 2004.

Baird, W. David. *Peter Pitchlynn: Chief of the Choctaws.* Civilization of the American Indian 116. Norman: University of Oklahoma Press, 1972.

Baker, T. Lindsay, and Julie P. Baker, eds. *The WPA Oklahoma Slave Narratives.* Norman: University of Oklahoma Press, 1996.

Bender, Norman J. "'We Surely Gave Them an Uplift': Taylor F. Ealy and the Mission School for Freedmen." *Chronicles of Oklahoma* 61 (1983): 180–93.

Berthrong, Donald J. *The Cheyenne and Arapaho Ordeal: Reservation and Agency Life in the Indian Territory, 1875–1907.* Norman: University of Oklahoma Press, 1976.

Bobroff, Kenneth H. "Retelling Allotment: Indian Property Rights and the Myth of Common Ownership." *Vanderbilt Law Review* 54, no. 4 (2001): 1559–623.

Bonnifield, Paul. "The Choctaw Nation on the Eve of the Civil War." *Journal of the West* 12, no. 3 (1973): 386–402.

Brown, Loren N. "The Appraisal of the Lands of the Choctaws and Chickasaws by the Dawes Commission." *Chronicles of Oklahoma* 22, no. 2 (1944): 177–91.

———. "The Choctaw-Chickasaw Court Citizens." *Chronicles of Oklahoma* 16, no. 4 (1938): 425–43.

———. "The Dawes Commission." *Chronicles of Oklahoma* 9, no. 1 (1931): 71–105.

Bryce, J. Y. "Judge Overton Love." *Chronicles of Oklahoma* 4, no. 3 (1926): 288–91.

Burton, Jeffrey. *Indian Territory and the United States, 1866–1906: Courts, Government, and the Movement for Oklahoma Statehood.* Legal History of North America 1. Norman: University of Oklahoma Press, 1995.

Carlson, Leonard A. *Indians, Bureaucrats and the Land: The Dawes Act and the Decline of Indian Farming.* Westport, Conn.: Greenwood, 1981.

Carter, Kent. *The Dawes Commission and the Allotment of the Five Civilized Tribes, 1893–1914.* Orem, Utah: Ancestry.com, 1999.

Cashin, Edward J. *Guardians of the Valley: Chickasaws in Colonial South Carolina and Georgia.* Columbia: University of South Carolina Press, 2009.

Champagne, Duane. *Social Order and Political Change: Constitutional Governments among the Cherokee, the Choctaw, the Chickasaw, and the Creek.* Stanford, Calif: Stanford University Press, 1992.

Cobb, Amanda J. *Listening to Our Grandmothers' Stories: The Bloomfield Academy for Chickasaw Females, 1852–1949.* Lincoln: University of Nebraska Press, 2000.

Cooper, Douglas. "A Journal Kept by Douglas Cooper on an Expedition by a Company of Chickasaws in Quest of Comanche Indians." Edited by Grant Foreman. *Chronicles of Oklahoma* 5, no. 4 (1927): 381–90.

Corbitt, D. C., and Roberta Corbitt, eds. "Papers from the Spanish Archives relating to Tennessee and the Old Southwest, 1783–1800." *East Tennessee Historical Society Publications* 29 (1957): 141–60.

Cushman, Horatio Bardwell. *History of the Choctaw, Chickasaw and Natchez Indians*. New York: Russell & Russell, 1972.

Davis, Caroline. "Education of the Chickasaws, 1856–1907." *Chronicles of Oklahoma* 15, no. 4 (1937): 415–48.

Day, James M., and Dorman H. Winfrey, eds. *Indian Papers of Texas and the Southwest, 1825–1916*. 5 vols. Austin: Pemberton, 1969.

Dean, Christopher C. *Letters on the Chickasaw and Osage Missions*. Missionary Series, Osage Mission, 9. Boston: Massachusetts Sabbath School Society, 1833.

Debo, Angie. *And Still the Waters Run: The Betrayal of the Five Civilized Tribes*. Princeton, N.J.: Princeton University Press, 1973.

Denson, Andrew. *Demanding the Cherokee Nation: Indian Autonomy and American Culture, 1830–1900*. Indians of the Southeast. Lincoln: University of Nebraska Press, 2004.

Foreman, Caroline T. "Education among the Chickasaw Indians." *Chronicles of Oklahoma* 15, no. 2 (1937): 139–65.

Foreman, Grant. *The Five Civilized Tribes*. Norman: University of Oklahoma Press, 1934.

Gibson, Arrell Morgan. *The Chickasaws*. Civilization of the American Indian 109. Norman: University of Oklahoma Press, 1971.

Gibson, Arrell Morgan, and Victor E. Harlow. *The History of Oklahoma*. Norman: University of Oklahoma Press, 1984.

Gideon, D. C. *Indian Territory, Descriptive, Biographical, and Genealogical, Including the Landed Estates, County Seats, etc., etc., with a General History of the Territory*. New York: Lewis, 1901.

Glisan, Rodney. *Journal of Army Life*. San Francisco: A. L. Bancroft, 1874.

Grafton, B. F. *Argument of B. F. Grafton, Delivered January 24, 1879, before the Committee on Territories of the United States Senate in Opposition to Any Legislation That Will in Anywise Interfere with the Five Civilized Tribes Inhabiting the Indian Territory, or Annul Their Present Tribal Organizations, or Their Respective Legislatures or Judiciaries, or Their Rights,*

Laws, Privileges, or Customs, as Solemnly Guaranteed by Treaty Stipulations. Washington, D.C.: Government Printing Office, 1879.

Green, Richard. *Chickasaw Lives.* Ada, Okla: Chickasaw Press, 2007.

Gregg, Josiah. *Commerce of the Prairies.* Edited by Max Moorhead. American Exploration and Travel. Norman: University of Oklahoma Press, 1954.

Hays, Robert G. *A Race at Bay:* New York Times *Editorials on "The Indian Problem," 1860–1900.* Carbondale: Southern Illinois University Press, 1997.

Hitchcock, Ethan Allen. *A Traveler in Indian Territory: The Journal of Ethan Allen Hitchcock, Late Major-General in the United States Army.* Edited by Grant Foreman. Cedar Rapids, Iowa: Torch, 1987.

Hochtritt, James Gribble. "Rural Cherokees, Chickasaws, Choctaws, Creeks, and Seminoles in Oklahoma during the Great Depression." Ph.D. diss., University of Oklahoma, 2000.

Holt, Marilyn Irvin. *Indian Orphanages.* Lawrence: University Press of Kansas, 2001.

Hudson, Charles M. *The Southeastern Indians.* Knoxville: University of Tennessee Press, 1976.

Jackson, Joe. C. "Summer Normals in Indian Territory After 1898." *Chronicles of Oklahoma* 37, no. 3 (1959): 307–29.

James, Parthena Louise. "The White Threat in the Chickasaw Nation." *Chronicles of Oklahoma* 46, no. 1 (1968): 75–85.

Johnson, Neil R., and C. Neil Kingsley. *The Chickasaw Rancher.* Boulder: University Press of Colorado, 2001.

Johnston, Douglas. *Argument on Behalf of the Chickasaw Nation against the Reopening of the Choctaw and Chickasaw Citizenship Rolls.* Washington, D.C.: Government Printing Office, 1910.

Kappler, Charles Joseph, and United States. *Indian Treaties, 1778–1883.* New York: Interland, 1972.

Kidwell, Clara Sue. *The Choctaws in Oklahoma: From Tribe to Nation, 1855–1970.* American Indian Law and Policy 2. Norman: University of Oklahoma Press, 2007.

Krauthamer, Barbara. "In Their 'Native Country': Freedpeople's Understandings of Culture and Citizenship in the Choctaw and Chickasaw Nations." In *Crossing Waters, Crossing Worlds,* edited by Tiya Miles and Sharon P. Holland. Durham, N.C.: Duke University Press, 2006.

LaVere, David. *Contrary Neighbors: Southern Plains and Removed Indians in Indian Territory.* Norman: University of Oklahoma Press, 2000.

———, ed. *Life among the Texas Indians: The WPA Narratives*. Elma Dill Russell Spencer Series in the West and Southwest 18. College Station: Texas A & M University Press, 2006.

Lewis, Monte Ross. "Chickasaw Removal: Betrayal of the Beloved Warriors, 1794–1844." Ph.D. diss., North Texas State University, 1981.

Littlefield, Daniel F. *The Cherokee Freedmen: From Emancipation to American Citizenship*. Contributions in Afro-American and African Studies 40. Westport, Conn.: Greenwood, 1978.

———. *The Chickasaw Freedmen: A People without a Country*. Contributions in Afro-American and African Studies 54. Westport, Conn.: Greenwood, 1980.

Litton, Gaston L., ed. "Notes and Documents: The Negotiations Leading to the Chickasaw-Choctaw Agreement, January 17, 1837." *Chronicles of Oklahoma* 17, no. 4 (1939): 417–27.

Lovegrove, Michael W. "Douglas Henry Johnston and the Chickasaw Nation, 1898–1939." Ph.D. diss., University of Oklahoma, 1999.

Marcy, Randolph Barnes. *Marcy and the Gold Seekers: The Journal of Captain R. B. Marcy, with an Account of the Gold Rush over the Southern Route*. Edited by Grant Foreman. Norman: University of Oklahoma Press, 1939.

———. *Thirty Years of Army Life on the Border*. Philadelphia: Lippincott, 1963.

McLoughlin, William Gerald. *After the Trail of Tears: The Cherokees' Struggle for Sovereignty, 1839–1880*. Chapel Hill: University of North Carolina Press, 1993.

Meserve, Charles F. *The Dawes Commission and the Five Civilized Tribes of Indian Territory*. Philadelphia: Office of the Indian Rights Association, 1896.

Meserve, John Bartlett. "Governor Benjamin Franklin Overton and Governor Benjamin Crooks Burney." *Chronicles of Oklahoma* 16, no. 2 (1938): 221–33.

———. "Governor Cyrus Harris." *Chronicles of Oklahoma* 15, no. 4 (1937): 373–86.

———. "Governor William Leander Byrd." *Chronicles of Oklahoma* 12, no. 4 (1934): 432–43.

Miner, H. Craig. *The Corporation and the Indian: Tribal Sovereignty and Industrial Civilization in Indian Territory, 1865–1907*. Columbia: University of Missouri Press, 1976.

Moore, John H. *The Cheyenne*. Peoples of America. Cambridge, Mass: Blackwell, 1996.

National Indian Law Library and United States. *Landmark Indian Law Cases.* AALL Publications Series 65. Buffalo, N.Y.: W. S. Hein, 2002.

Nye, Wilbur Sturtevant, and William S. Soule. *Plains Indian Raiders: The Final Phases of Warfare from the Arkansas to the Red River.* Norman: University of Oklahoma Press, 1968.

O'Beirne, Harry F. *Leaders and Leading Men of the Indian Territory, with Interesting Biographical Sketches of Choctaws and Chickasaws.* Chicago: American Publishers Association, 1891.

Perdue, Theda. *Nations Remembered: An Oral History of the Five Civilized Tribes, 1865–1907.* Contributions in Ethnic Studies 1. Westport, Conn: Greenwood, 1980.

Roark, Michael O. *Nineteenth Century Population Distributions of the Five Civilized Tribes in Indian Territory, Oklahoma.* Syracuse, N.Y.: Department of Geography, Syracuse University, 1976.

Roff, Joe T. "Reminiscences of Early Days in the Chickasaw Nation." *Chronicles of Oklahoma* 13, no. 2 (1935): 169–90.

St. Jean, Wendy. "After Removal: Class and Ethnic Divisions in the Chickasaw Nation." *Journal of Chickasaw History* 5, no. 2 (1999): 7–20

———. "'You Have the Land, I Have the Cattle': Intermarried Whites and the Chickasaw Range Lands." *Chronicles of Oklahoma* 78 (Summer 2000): 182–95.

Texas State Library, Dorman H. Winfrey, and James M. Day. *Texas Indian Papers.* Austin: Texas State Library, 1959.

United States. *Annual Report of the Commissioner of Indian Affairs to the Secretary of the Interior.* Washington, D.C.: Government Printing Office, 1843–1907.

———. *Annual Report of the Commission to the Five Civilized Tribes to the Secretary of the Interior.* Muscogee, Indian Territory: Department of the Interior, Commission to the Five Civilized Tribes, 1894.

———. *Annual Report of the United States Inspector for Indian Territory, Together with the Reports of the Superintendents of Schools in That Territory to the Secretary of the Interior for the Fiscal Year Ended June 30, 1899.* Washington, D.C.: Government Printing Office, 1899.

———. *Citizenship of Five Civilized Tribes: Communication from the Assistant Secretary of the Interior to Hon. Robert L. Owen, Submitting a List of Names of Persons Apparently Equitably Entitled to Enrollment on the Rolls of the Various Tribes Composing the Five Civilized Tribes of Oklahoma, Be-*

ing Senate Document 472, Sixty-third Congress. Washington, D.C.: Government Printing Office, 1914.

———. *Leasing Lands of the Five Civilized Tribes: Report (to Accompany S. 1874).* Washington, D.C.: U.S. Government Printing Office, 1934.

———. *Regulations for Tribal Indian Schools among the Five Civilized Tribes.* Washington, D.C.: Government Printing Office, 1906.

———. *Report of the Commission Appointed to Negotiate with the Five Civilized Tribes of Indians, Known as the Dawes Commission.* Washington, D.C.: Government Printing Office, 1895.

———. *Report of the Commissioner to the Five Civilized Tribes to the Secretary of the Interior.* Washington, D.C.: Government Printing Office, 1906–10.

———. *Report of the Superintendent for the Five Civilized Tribes of Oklahoma.* Washington, D.C.: Government Printing Office, 1915.

———. *Reports of the Commissioner to the Five Civilized Tribes* [1893/94–1919/20]. Arlington, Va: University Publications of America, 1975.

———. *Rights of Indians to Impose Taxes.* 45th Cong., 2nd sess., S. Exec. Doc. 74, 21.

———. *Survey of Conditions of the Indians in the United States: Hearings before a Subcommittee of the Committee on Indian Affairs, United States Senate.* 71st Cong., 2nd sess. Washington, D.C.: Government Printing Office, 1931.

United States and John Coggswell Conner. *Outrages Committed by Indians on Western and Southwestern Frontiers. (To Accompany H. Res. No. 288.) May 16, 1870.—Referred to the Committee on Indian Affairs and Ordered to Be Printed.* United States Congressional Serial Set 1433. 1870.

United States, Walter Adair Duncan, Roach Young, and Isaac Charles Parker. *Remarks by Walter A. Duncan, Roach Young and Judge I. C. Parker, before the House Judiciary Committee on Change of Government of the Five Civilized Tribes and Remonstrance of Indian Delegates.* Washington, D.C.: Government Printing Office, 1974.

United States and S. B. Maxey. *In the Senate of the United States.* Washington, D.C.: Government Printing Office, 1887.

United States and Henry Moore Teller. *Five Civilized Tribes of Indians Report.* Washington, D.C.: U.S. Government Printing Office, 1894.

Unrau, William E. *Mixed-Bloods and Tribal Dissolution: Charles Curtis and the Quest for Indian Identity.* Lawrence: University Press of Kansas, 1989.

Warren, Harry. "Some Chickasaw Chiefs and Prominent Men." *Publications of Mississippi Historical Society* 8 (1904): 555–70.

Wickett, Murray R. *Contested Territory: Whites, Native Americans, and African Americans in Oklahoma, 1865–1907.* Baton Rouge: Louisiana State University Press, 2000.

Wilkins, David E. *American Indian Sovereignty and the U.S. Supreme Court: The Masking of Justice.* Austin: University of Texas Press, 1997.

Wright, Muriel H. "Brief Outline of the Choctaw and Chickasaw Nations in Indian Territory, 1820 to 1860." *Chronicles of Oklahoma* 7, no. 4 (1929): 388–420.

———. "Wapanucka Academy, Chickasaw Nation." *Chronicles of Oklahoma* 12, no. 4 (1934): 402–31.

Yarborough, James Martin. "The Transition of the Chickasaw Indians from an Organized Nation to a Part of a State." Master's thesis, Oklahoma Agricultural and Mechanical College, 1938.

Yarbrough, Fay A. *Race and the Cherokee Nation: Sovereignty in the Nineteenth Century.* Philadelphia: University of Pennsylvania Press, 2008.

Young, Mary Elizabeth. *Redskins, Ruffleshirts and Rednecks: Indian Allotments in Alabama and Mississippi, 1830–1860.* Civilization of the American Indian. Norman: University of Oklahoma Press, 1961.

Zissu, Erik March. *Blood Matters: The Five Civilized Tribes and the Search for Unity in the Twentieth Century.* New York: Routledge, 2001.

Index